The Successful
Herb Gardener

The Successful
Herb Gardener

GROWING AND USING HERBS—QUICKLY AND EASILY

SALLY ROTH

COUNTRY LIVING
GARDENER

HEARST BOOKS   NEW YORK

Country Living Gardener
Editor-in-Chief Diana Gold Murphy
Horticulture Editor Ruth Rogers Clausen

Created and produced by Carroll & Brown Limited

Editor Charlotte Beech
Managing Art Editor Adelle Morris
Design Assistant Roland Codd

Hearst Books
959 Eighth Avenue
New York, N.Y. 10019

Library of Congress Cataloging-in-Publication Data

Roth, Sally.
     Country living gardener : the successful herb gardener / Sally Roth.
          p. cm.
     "Country living gardener."
     ISBN 1-58816-074-2
     1. Herb gardening. 2. Herbs. I. Country living gardener. II. Title.

SB351.H5 R68 2001
635'.7–dc21

2001016790

Reproduced by Emirates in Dubai
Printed and bound by Imago in Singapore

1 2 3 4 5 6 7 8 9 10

The information in this book is intended to increase your
knowledge about herbs, but is not intended to be medical
advice or present a course of personalized treatment.
There may be risks involved with herbal remedies and
therefore before starting use of any herbal remedy, you
should consult your own healthcare practitioner.

www.cl-gardener.com

Contents

INTRODUCTION why herbs? 6

1 planning your garden 8

a home for herbs 9 indoors 10 herbs in containers 11 herbs in gardens 13 informal gardens 14 formal gardens 17 theme gardens 19 special places 21

the four essentials 24 climate 24 light 26 soil 26 drainage 27

preparing and improving the site 28 making the bed 28

choosing plants 30 savvy shopping 30

2 planting 31

how to plant your herbs 32 from the beginning 32 companion planting 37 attracting beneficial insects 38

tools and equipment 39 a gardener's toolbox 39

3 maintaining and propagating 41

tending your herbs 42 weed control 42 minimizing weeds 43 mulch 44 watering 45 fertilizing 45

winter protection 46 transplanting indoors 46

pests and diseases 48 organic controls 48

propagation 50 seed 50 division 51 cuttings 53 layering 54

4 harvesting, storing, and using herbs 55

useful parts 56 harvesting 56 preparing and storing herbs for use 59

putting herbs to use 62 culinary magic 62 medicinal use 66 home decor 69 cosmetic preparations 72 herbs that encourage wildlife 74

5 herb directory 75 more than 100 herbs arranged alphabetically by latin names

INDEX 188

ACKNOWLEDGMENTS 192

why herbs?

As beautiful as any plants in the garden, herbs are steeped in centuries of history and romance. A plant's usefulness is what classifies it as an herb, whether it's a sprig of thyme simmered in a stew or a few stems of lavender laid between the linens. The uses for herbs are almost as endless as the variety of these plants. Every culture has its favorites, which it uses to flavor food and drink, heal a multitude of human ailments, make the home smell better, discourage pests, and even improve personal appearance or smooth the skin.

Knowing the stories behind herbs and using them in everyday activities makes these plants a very personal part of your garden. But usefulness is only part of the reason herbs are favorites in gardens. These plants are also beautiful, with delightfully fragrant leaves and often delicate flowers. Because many popular herbs have lovely foliage in soft grays and greens and understated flowers, you'll find that combining them is simple: everything looks good together, so designing an attractive garden is easy. You can slip herbs in among ornamentals, or keep them handy in a special patch of, say, culinary herbs or a tea garden. Growing herbs can also give you a healthier garden, thanks to their pest-repelling ability. What's more, their blossoms attract beneficial insects, which will patrol other parts of your garden to destroy harmful insects.

So many plants have been used as herbs around the globe that, chances are, your yard already includes a plentiful sampling of them. Those dandelions that dot the green grass of spring, for instance, are actually escapees from the medicine chests of European settlers, who brought them along for their cure-almost-all properties. The flamboyant hibiscus flowers that pretty up your patio in summer can similarly be called herbs, because they were once used in order to soothe a nervous stomach.

Use this book to help you decide which herbs to choose, where to plant them, and how to care for them so they enjoy a long and useful life. Browse through the directory in chapter 5 to discover old favorites and intriguing new herbs to try in your own yard. You'll learn how to harvest and store your herbs, too, so that you can enjoy using them in the many recipes and project ideas you'll come across in these pages. One word of caution: Gardening with herbs is so much fun, it can quickly turn you into a dedicated collector. Experiment with just a few of these fascinating plants, and you will open the door to a gardening hobby that will last a lifetime.

Herbs are full of surprises to add a little zest to your life—a simple summer dessert can become an unusual and unexpected delight in a decorative ice bowl, complete with edible chive flowers, cucumber, and mint encased in its walls

1

planning your garden

Starting an herb garden is often as casual as bringing home that first small pot of lavender. Soon there's a plant of rosemary nearby, and an edging of creeping thyme sneaking out along the stepping stones. That's a fine beginning, but for the most satisfying garden, it helps to do a bit of daydreaming before you pick up the trowel and load up the trunk.

a home for herbs

No matter how small or how grand your garden, there's a place for herbs—which is a good thing, because herb gardens have a habit of expanding as you come across exciting new plants to try. Read on to discover how to make the most of your garden space.

Herbs thrive in all kinds of settings. They flourish in containers as well as planted in the garden, can snuggle into niches between stepping stones or fill entire beds. Start by thinking about how you plan to use your herbs. If cooking is high on the list, you'll want the culinary herbs near the kitchen door so you can snip a few stems of parsley or chives without making a major expedition. If you're planning to decorate your home with herbs in dried arrangements or potpourri, you'll want those herbs where you can easily reach them, perhaps in a special cutting garden, or at least near a path.

Notice which gardens in this book appeal to you most. Is your eye attracted to the cottage-style jumble, the simplicity of plants in classic pots, or the intricate curves of a knot garden? Many herb gardeners like to keep their collection in a separate herbs-only garden, a place that quickly becomes a gathering of old and new plant friends. Others choose to mingle herbs and flowers, planting parsley or thyme as an edging to ornamentals. Most of us mix it up, keeping some favorite herbs in their own space and moving others to any spot that seems fitting. You'll find an abundance of ideas in the following pages to help you decide what kinds of gardens suit your style.

Practical considerations are vital, too. Herbs originally hail from regions all around the world, so you'll find many plants that will thrive in your yard, no matter where your garden is. Select those that suit your climate and your growing conditions, just as you would any other garden plant. Sun and well-drained soil are the basics for many herbs, but others will thrive in shade, heavy clay, or even particularly wet soils.

basil

bay

cardamom

chives

dill

lemon verbena

parsley

rosemary

sage

thyme

indoors

A sunny windowsill gives you enough growing room to keep a fine collection of cooking herbs for the kitchen: parsley, sage, rosemary, and thyme, perhaps oregano for livening up the pizza and chives for Sunday-morning scrambled eggs. It's a cook's dream in just 18 inches of shelf space. Basil is an easy candidate for windowsill culture, because the seeds sprout fast and the plants grow to usable size in a matter of weeks.

There is no need to stop with the kitchen, either. Use lavender or scented geraniums as a natural air freshener for your living room, or in the bath, where you can add a few leaves to steaming water for a fragrant, relaxing soak.

If you live in a cold-winter area, move tender potted herbs indoors to enjoy as houseplants on a sunny, glassed-in porch or under full-spectrum grow lights. Narrow, plastic windowbox liners fit on many indoor sills, making it a simple matter to grow annual herbs, like bright-flowered, peppery-tasting nasturtiums, or feathery dill from seed.

TIPS FOR SUCCESSFUL INDOOR HERB GARDENING

■ Give plants as much light as possible—south-facing windows or artificial grow lights are ideal.

■ Buy young potted plants for best success. Plants moved in from the garden may have difficulty adjusting; transplant any divisions or cuttings to pots during the summer, and leave them for a few weeks before the indoor move.

■ Keep herbs away from heat sources.

■ Pinch to keep plants bushy and compact.

■ Use lightweight plastic pots, so you can easily move them for cleaning or to catch more light.

■ Protect floors and windowsills by placing waterproof trays underneath pots.

If you're lucky enough to have a heated sun-room or a wall consisting of mostly windows, the increased warmth and light will expand your options. Grow lemongrass or lemon verbena for flavored teas, or try a tumble of German chamomile with its delicate, white daisies. For a specimen plant, try hibiscus, whose pretty petals add color and flavor to iced beverages. Greenhouses will also protect plants in winter.

herbs in containers

Growing your plants in containers is a convenient and satisfying way to get started with outdoor herb gardening, and also adds visual excitement to any garden. For a small investment in a container, potting mix, and plants, you can have a handy windowbox, beautiful hanging basket, or a garden centerpiece in place in less than an hour.

POTS

Potted plants are attention-grabbers in the garden, acting as focal points that draw the eye. To make the pot stand out even further, you could

 10 best herbs for pots

bay   cardamom   lavender   lemon grass   lemon verbena   pansies   rosemary   sage   scented geraniums   thyme

10 best herbs for windowboxes

aloe vera

artemisias

chamomile

lavenders

lemon verbena

Madagascar
periwinkle

pansies

sage

santolina

scented
geraniums

set it on a wall, post, or doorstep, or give it a gentle boost by perching it on top of bricks or an overturned pot. Use large pots to flank a gateway or doorstep, or elevate a big pot among the exuberant herbs of an informal garden to help create a sense of control.

Light, fast-draining potting soil is ideal for the roots of many herbs, including popular lavender, oregano, thyme, and scented geraniums. Add a few scoops of compost or some granulated water-holding polymer gel beads to reduce your watering chores. A water-soluble balanced fertilizer or organic supplement such as fish emulsion, if applied weekly, will keep your potted herbs growing vigorously.

You can combine herbs of similar cultural needs, plant a sampler of different kinds of the same herb (various lavenders or thymes, for instance), or use just one herb. Fill the container with potting mix, then play with your plants until you like the arrangement. Slip them out of their starter pots one at a time, scoop out a hole, and shoehorn them in tightly. Leave 2 inches above the soil line to help prevent water overflowing.

WINDOWBOXES

Irresistibly charming, windowboxes are an appealing addition to your home because they bring the garden right up to your walls. The conditions are demanding, though, so you'll need to choose herbs that can survive in a difficult site. On the sunny side of your house, windowboxes

can create almost desert conditions for your herbs. The roots have little insulating soil to protect them from the full force of the sun, and the plants get extra heat reflected from the nearby glass and wall. Plastic liners are a sneaky way to keep windowboxes looking good. You can slip them out in seconds to give tired plants a rest and slide in fresh replacements.

Plan to water a windowbox at least once a day in summer, preferably in the morning so that roots have enough moisture to draw on during the heat of high noon. Water-holding polymer gel beads added to the soil at planting time, or self-watering windowboxes can make life easier for your plants, and you, by providing a backup source of water when you can't get to the hose.

HANGING BASKETS

Fill hanging baskets with mounding or upright plants in the center to balance the pot visually, and finish the arrangement with cascading herbs around the edge to make it look graceful. As in other plantings, you can stick to herbs alone or blend other plants into the design. A lacy collar of German chamomile, for example, adds a dainty contrast to the large flowers of petunias, and also looks beautiful with the scalloped gray foliage of apple-scented geranium. Hens-and-chicks make an intriguing basket when you stud them around the sides and bottom of an open-frame container lined with spaghnum moss and filled with potting mix. They will soon cover every inch of empty space with clusters of highly textured rosettes.

Read catalogs and plant tags carefully to find good herb varieties, or cultivars, for your hanging baskets. Depending on the cultivar, herbs such as rosemary and thyme may be upright in growth habit or they may sprawl and spread—these are the attributes you want for your basket.

Plant and care for hanging baskets as you would herbs in pots, watering them frequently and fertilizing about once a week.

TOPIARY

A neatly trimmed cone or ball of greenery is the perfect finishing touch for a formal or semi-formal garden, as the hand of the gardener is very much in control. Known as topiary, these decoratively pruned plants also make striking table centerpieces. Any herb with a single main stem and a branching habit of growth may be trained.

You can buy topiary-grown herbs in nurseries and garden centers, or you can make your own. Start with a young herb, the bushiest you can find. Prune it into the basic shape you want, then wait a few weeks to let new branches form. Pinch or snip off the first set of leaves from each tip to encourage more branching. Once the plant has dense new foliage, fine-tune it by selectively snipping off tender branch tips. Water as normal but be generous with nitrogen-boosting fertilizer.

As the plant grows, maintain the shape by snipping off any wayward shoots as they appear

herbs in gardens

Spend a few minutes considering the general garden design principles of contrasting or complementing texture, shape, and color, and you can use a palette of herbs to paint a garden portrait as beautiful as any ornamental planting. Foliage is an outstanding attribute of many herbs, often with deliciously soft or fine texture and a gentle range of grays and greens. Intersperse bold-leaved herbs, such as chicory or Joe Pye weed, among daintier garden neighbors, for a textural contrast that makes both partners more pleasing to the eye. Slip in an upright citizen like angelica or mullein for a vertical exclamation point among more relaxed company.

ALONE AND AS PARTNERS

An all-herb garden is always satisfying, because the plants share a common bond that ties them together: they're all useful for one thing or another. Many enthusiasts find pleasure in an herb garden arranged by type of use rather than ornamental design: all cooking herbs, for instance, or all curative herbs.

Adding herbs to ornamental plantings broadens their contribution to the garden. The dramatic deep red foliage of fennel or perilla, for example, adds a valuable deep note to a bed of pastel flowers. Lots of favorite garden flowers are really herbs at heart: roses, for example have many

practical uses beyond looking beautiful. Throughout this book, you'll find photos and suggestions to inspire new ways to mix and mingle your herbs and flowers, whether you grow them alone or to add flair to flowerbeds.

informal gardens

A relaxed attitude comes naturally to herbs, many of which will spread, sprawl, or creep instead of staying in tidy clumps. They're well suited to the casual style of informal gardens, therefore, where the lines of borders are more loose and curving, and the plants can easily blend into each other.

BORDERS

Plant herbs in borders according to their height and habit, whether you're planning a herbs-only garden or you want to mix them in with your favorite ornamentals. Tall, stout herbs with large leaves, such as angelica and Joe Pye weed, are best positioned toward the back of borders, where they won't block the sun or your view of the shorter plants. Some tall herbs, especially annuals such as dill and caraway, have small leaves and an open habit, making them easy to see through. Plant these in the middle or even in the front of a bed or border, where their lightweight texture won't get lost in the crowd. Herbs of mounded habit, for example sage or thyme,

the kitchen garden

Keep your most-used culinary herbs close at hand by growing them in pots or a raised bed close to your kitchen door. Start with the basics—parsley, chives, dill, thyme, and anything else you and your family like. Experiment with unfamiliar herbs, too, perhaps tarragon for Friday fish dinners or cilantro to jazz up a salsa. When the possibilities are right in arm's reach, you'll be much more inclined to liven up the menu. Be sure to label each plant so friends and family members can help with the harvesting.

should go in the middle, while creepers and low growers, such as chamomile or creeping thyme, look best edging the bed.

It's hard to make mistakes when combining herbs, but do try to avoid inviting aggressive spreaders, such as mint, tansy, and goldenrod, into your beds and borders. Keep these in a separate area where they can fill the bed themselves or jostle with other strong characters for space.

RAISED BEDS

These allow you to offer herbs better soil and drainage than they would find at ground level, but they also offer advantages beyond the practical. Their straight lines add control to the billow of herbs within, and the extra height garners atten-

tion. They also raise herbs closer to nose level for easy sampling, and are thus convenient for those of us with limited mobility, because they reduce the need for stooping and kneeling.

Most herbs will decline quickly when they are surrounded by dense, wet soil. If your garden is plagued with heavy clay or other slow-to-drain soil, consider lifting your herbs out of harm's way. Building a raised bed for them can solve the drainage difficulties of most herbs, as their roots will usually go no deeper than 6 inches. This means you can create plenty of extra gardening space on top of a driveway, patio, or other paving.

To make a frame, use decay-resistant landscaping timbers, anchoring the corners with sturdy metal supports available at home-supply

Unrestrained herbs create a lush composition, weaving together to make a garden seem long-established

Aromatic rosemary thrives in the kind of arid mountainside conditions that leave most plants gasping for moisture

COTTAGE GARDENS

The romance of an old-fashioned cottage garden goes hand in hand with herbs, many of which have been at home for centuries in humble dooryard gardens. Recreate the ambience by adding self-sowing herbs that will return year after year to find their place in among your flowers.

Some herbs seed themselves so freely that they can quickly become pesky in a planned garden. But in the informal, ever-changing style of the cottage garden, this characteristic is welcomed. Herbs and flowers here need to produce plenty of progeny, or they stand no chance among the other seedlings springing to life each year. If certain herbs begin to overwhelm the garden, however, pull out or hoe off any unwanted plants.

stores and garden centers. Fill the frame with purchased topsoil, or improve your soil's texture by mixing it with liberal amounts of coarse sand, compost, peat moss, or other organic materials.

Use a single raised bed to corral a bunch of kitchen herbs, spotlight favorites, or lay out several beds with paths running between them. The space in a raised bed is limited, so plant well-behaved herbs that will not spread too quickly.

ROCK GARDENS

It may look inhospitable to us, but a stony, thin-soiled spot actually feels just like home to many herbs, which thrive in the excellent drainage of a rock garden. The stones also invite roots to grow among and under them, where they will remain cool and moist. Their contrasting color and texture will also make your herbs really stand out.

Choose plants that spread slowly or stay in well-behaved clumps for your rock garden, so that your tapestry of herbs remains as you planned it, instead of being swallowed up by a dominant spreading plant. Look for herbs with gray or silvery foliage—a clue that the plant will thrive in the fast-draining soil of a rock garden.

10 best herbs for cottage gardens

borage   caraway   chicory   dill   evening primrose   foxglove   lemon balm   poppies   Queen Anne's lace   shepherd's purse

formal gardens

The guiding hand is very evident within a formal herb garden, with plants growing in a well-defined space. The simplest formal garden consists of well-groomed beds set off by wide paths and stretches of lawn. Select neatly shaped, slower-growing herbs, instead of those that spread rapidly, to maintain the sense of formality. Surprisingly, formal gardens usually require less maintenance than casual styles, because each plant sticks to its assigned place.

A formal style also allows room for creativity— try your hand at planting an herb garden in the shape of a wheel or an intricate knot, or section a rectangular plot into a geometric garden, or parterre. If you are planting a low hedge or a knot, turn to small-leaved herbs with a dense branching pattern, which can quickly be trained into shape. Plant your formal herb bed where you can admire it from above, from a deck or high window.

KNOT GARDENS

To weave a fanciful knot from herbs of contrasting color, begin by planning on paper. Once you have a design that satisfies your eye and shows where each strand of the knot goes, mark the pattern on prepared soil with a hoe and set in the young plants. Try to include at least one contrasting color: perhaps a thread of red-leaved sage or bright silver artemisia. Plant them closely and shear once a month during the first season to promote dense, compact growth.

To prepare the wheel garden bed, remove weeds and rake soil smooth and level before laying bricks

Mark segments and scrape out channels in which to lay bricks. Set them in place, pushing them firmly into the soil

Use a pitchfork to work in some gravel to give your herbs the fast-draining soil that their roots will flourish best in

Plant each segment, spacing plants a few inches more closely than the recommended guidelines for a faster finished effect

WHEEL

Picture a pie, with each wedge a different herb, and you have the basic form of a wheel garden. You can also dot the center with a neat, mounded, or tall plant, or edge the rim with a low-growing herb such as chamomile. Add definition by edging each wedge with a ground-hugging herb, such as creeping thyme, or lay a flat double row of bricks as the spokes. The wheel design works well for small kitchen gardens, because you won't have to search for your frequently used plants.

PARTERRE

Blocks or triangles of herbs laid within a rectangular or square outline create a parterre. This framework is great to showcase a collection of herbs, such as various varieties of thymes' or basils. You'll find a symmetrical arrangement, with both halves of the garden mirroring each other in outline, most pleasing to the eye. Use herbs of contrasting foliage color and texture in alternating segments of the wheel.

The visual strength of straight lines means that even the simplest design, say, four intersecting triangles, can be a delight. You can separate each section from its neighbors with a row of brick if you like, or else leave a strip of earth in between to create the borders.

theme gardens

The world of herbs is an extremely large one, with hundreds of possibilities lined up on garden center tables or tempting you from the pages of a catalog. Choosing to plan your garden around a particular theme is a great way to focus your exploration by limiting the selection to herbs that fit a certain category.

The choice of theme is entirely up to you—for example, you may decide to start with a sampler of a dozen kinds of thyme, or go for various herbs that share a pleasant lemony fragrance, or plant herbs that will spice up your favorite style of cuisine. Spend a little time thinking about those aspects of herbs that appeal to you the most, as well as those that you find most intriguing, and use these as a basis upon which to build a theme garden that satisfies your interest.

culinary herbs for worldwide cuisines

ASIAN anise, cardamom, cayenne pepper, lemongrass

MEXICAN cayenne pepper, cilantro, garlic

ITALIAN basil, fennel, garlic, marjoram, oregano, parsley, rosemary, thyme

MIDDLE EASTERN cardamom, garlic, parsley, rosemary, saffron

GERMAN chives, dill, horseradish, sage, thyme

CULINARY

A pinch of this, a snip of that, and suddenly even leftovers get a fresh lease on life. Flavor-packed herbs are easy to grow and give you a generous yield even from a single plant. Plant a patch of culinary herbs near your kitchen door, and keep a collection in pots on the deck or patio to liven up grilled chicken and other tasty dishes.

MEDICINAL

Backed by generations of folklore, herbal remedies have made a comeback, with bottles of echinacea and aromatherapy potions around every corner. Many medicinal herbs are perfectly safe when used occasionally, but others pack a powerful punch. While there is good reason to be cautious (see page 70), a medicinal herb garden is still a great conversation piece and gives you a feeling of connection to the wise folks of old.

COSMETIC

It's easy to grow the basis for your own soaps, lotions, and hair rinses right in your own backyard. Use lavender to perfume a bottle of hand lotion, bring out the highlights in your blonde hair with a splash of chamomile rinse after shampooing, or soothe tired eyes with cotton puffs dipped in witch hazel. You'll find recipes and tips for making the most of your cosmetic herbs on page 72.

making sense of scented herbs

CITRUSY TANG beebalm, lemongrass, lemon balm, lemon basil, lemon verbena, lemon or orange-scented cultivars of thyme and scented geraniums

LICORICE SCENT anise, fennel, sweet cicely

PUNGENT OR MEDICINAL ODOR chervil, perilla, saffron, tansy, witch hazel

SWEET, FLOWERY, OR FRUITY AROMA burnet, chamomile, lavender, scented geraniums, sweet woodruff (when dried)

SCENTED HERBS

Delight your senses with a selection of fragrant herbs, arranged to highlight one favorite aroma or as a mixture of perfumes. Even the most fragrant herbs smell only faintly until a leaf is brushed or pinched to release the aromatic oils, so plant your scented garden where the leaves can be easily reached for sniffing.

There are three groups of scented herbs that could form the basis of an entire aromatic garden all by themselves. Cultivars of thyme, scented geraniums, and mints carry almost every type of perfume you can imagine, including chocolate, coconut, and nutmeg as well as lemon and peppermint. Their foliage and form vary too, so you can make a lovely display from just one group.

GROW A "FIRST AID KIT"

Try these simple, safe herbs in your medicinal garden.

- Keep a potted aloe plant on the kitchen windowsill and next to your outdoor grill for quick first aid for burns. Just split a juicy leaf and apply its thick, soothing gel to the skin.
- Sip chamomile tea to calm your senses before sleep.
- Sniff a freshly broken root of horseradish to instantly clear your stuffy sinuses.
- Nibble a leaf of peppermint to quiet an aching tummy. Or quickly remove cooking or tobacco odors from your hands by rubbing the fresh leaves between your fingers.

special places

Because herbs flourish so well in containers, they are perfect for adding a touch of portable greenery to outdoor living spaces like patios, decks, and rooftop gardens. Select sun-loving herbs for these gardens, which can take the full force of the sun's rays even when the heat and light is reflected from paved surfaces. Herbs with velvety or fuzzy leaves or foliage that is gray or silver lose less water to evaporation and are well suited for difficult sunny sites.

PATIOS

Bring your garden onto the patio by planting herbs in large pots, wooden half-barrels, formal boxes, or other containers. The larger the pot, the less quickly it dries out. Grouping containers also helps reduce evaporation. For minimal watering chores, plant aloe vera and hens-and-chicks, whose succulent leaves hold water in reserve.

Fragrant herbs add an extra sensory pleasure to outdoor gatherings. Culinary herbs are another good choice because you can use them to flavor outdoor meals. Edibles such as cayenne pepper or a trailing cucumber vine are other possibilities.

DECKS, BALCONIES, AND ROOFS

Plants add a welcoming touch to any outdoor space, giving it the romance of a garden even if there's no soil beneath your feet. Hang window-boxes from the railing of a deck or balcony, or dot a flat rooftop with faux terra cotta pots.

You'll want to choose plants that can stand up to heat, light, and wind, as well as grow vigorously in a limited amount of soil. Luckily, many herbs are born for such conditions, including favorites such as thymes and lavenders. Coddle your plants by adding water-holding polymer gel beads to the soil mix to ensure a constant source of moisture.

10 best herbs for patios, decks, and roof gardens

aloe vera   cayenne pepper   cucumber   hens-and-chicks   lavender   lemon verbena   morning glory   oregano   scented geraniums   thyme

Weight is a big consideration for plants in elevated places—a large clay pot filled with soil can weigh in at 50 pounds or more. Stick to lightweight plastic pots rather than heavy terra cotta or ceramic, and since herb roots usually stay in the top 6 to 8 inches of soil, fill the bottoms of large pots with non-biodegradable foam packing peanuts. Use a commercial soilless potting mix, which is lighter in weight than topsoil and provides the free drainage that herb roots prefer.

Before you fill your special area with potted herbs, remember that one large container needs less frequent watering than several small ones. Self-watering containers with a built-in reservoir for plants to draw on will also cut down on care.

LAWNS AND GROUNDCOVERS

Imagine walking barefoot across a swath of springy-soft creeping thyme, each step releasing a fresh burst of scent. It's a lovely image, and an easy project to undertake if you use ground-hugging herbs that spread thick and fast. Sprinkle a few flowering herbs into your lawn as well if you like the look; English daisies, German chamomile, self-heal, and violas will all add color to your fragrant footing. You can also place stepping stones among them if you want to avoid the possibility of wearing a path through your planting.

On steep slopes and other areas where you want to retire the lawnmower, groundcover herbs can do the job, filling in so thickly that they crowd

Plant groundcover in areas among your paving stones. It will spread onto the stones and exude its scent when stepped upon

Pry up your chosen pavers using a sturdy shovel and use a garden fork to mix in coarse sand and organic material

Plant herbs of a dense, low-growing habit, such as creeping thyme or mint, closely together within the allotted space

10 best herbs for groundcover

beebalm · chamomile · creeping thyme · ground ivy · mints · oregano · soapwort · sweet woodruff · wild strawberry · wooly thyme out potential weed problems. Groundcover herbs can be low growers like creeping thyme that form mats just a couple of inches high, or they may be plants of knee height or more, like beebalm. Look for herbs that expand vigorously from spreading roots, such as mints. In a garden situation, such an aggressive personality is unwelcome, but for covering ground, a tendency to take over is ideal.

Chamomile and creeping varieties of thyme will quickly weave together into a dense lawn, capable of standing up to light foot traffic

LOW HEDGES

A sense of enclosure makes a yard feel cozier, as well as defining areas for various activities. You can use herbs, trimmed or left to grow naturally, to establish low hedges around sitting areas or to guide the eye or the feet from one part of the garden to another. For a taller, more casual hedge, try flowering herbs such as valerian or hibiscus, which will form a relaxed row.

Plant herbs for hedges at intervals of about half the recommended distance for garden situations—so that their branches interweave to create a seamless wall. Shear them with electric hedge clippers two or three times a growing season to achieve a neat, formal look and to encourage interior branching.

NICHES

Herbs have a charming habit of snuggling their roots into cracks in paving and other niches. Take advantage of their resourcefulness by starting sprigs in paths and walls to create an appealing contrast to the solid surfaces around them.

Herbs can also hop into inviting cracks all by themselves, sprouting from self-sown seeds. Learn to recognize youthful poppies, thymes, and other herbs so that you can appreciate this serendipity instead of mistaking them for weeds.

paths Use a pencil or screwdriver to poke chamomile, wooly thyme, and other creeping thymes or low growers into the joints between bricks or stones. Make sure the roots are in contact with the sand between the paving, and spoon a bit more soil over them. Water with a gentle spray and they will quickly grab a roothold. Most herbs rebound quickly from sporadic footsteps, and will also release a delightful scent.

walls Use herbs to spill over the top of walls or wiggle into niches between the layers of stone. Cascading or prostrate varieties of rosemary, creeping thymes, and the charming rosettes of hens-and-chicks are good candidates as their roots can fit into tiny niches, finding moisture and sustenance behind the stones. For dry stone walls, built without mortar, use an old butter knife to slide soil into crevices to support the roots.

A screwdriver makes quick work of easing herbs into crevices

the four essentials

Choosing herbs that are at home in your garden is the key to success. Before you invite them in, take time to consider their cultural requirements—soil type, seasonal conditions, humidity, and the amount of rain and sun all determine which will grow best.

climate

Your climate is the number-one factor that should determine your choices, although even that is negotiable: by growing herbs in pots and wintering them indoors, you can succeed with tender herbs even in cold-winter areas.

The USDA Hardiness Zone system, based on average wintertime low temperatures, is the basic consideration in finding herbs suited to your area, as cold can be a killer. Read labels and catalog descriptions to find out the minimum USDA Hardiness Zone of the herbs you intend to plant. If you're unsure what zone you live in, call your USDA extension agent, listed in the blue pages of the phone book under county offices.

You can still grow tender herbs in cold areas by enjoying them as one-season plants, or by moving them indoors for the winter. If you want to try your

tender and tropical herbs

These warm-weather herbs shiver when freezing temperatures approach. Bring them indoors in early fall to prevent damage or death from cold. **anise, bay, blessed thistle, cardamom, cayenne pepper, ephedra, hibiscus, lemongrass, Madagascar periwinkle, periwinkle, rosemary, saw palmetto, scented geraniums**

Whether a spot is in the sun all day long, or your borders tend to hide in the shade, light should be a crucial factor in your choice of herbs

luck, you could plant any tender herbs in pots so that they're instantly portable when the weather begins to turn chilly.

Many catalogs and reference books have begun including the maximum recommended USDA Hardiness Zone, as well as the minimum. This is because many plants fail to thrive in the steamy summers of the Deep South or other warm-weather extremes.

As a rule of thumb, you can assume that plants that are sold at your local garden center or nursery are well adapted to your climate. When you start branching out a little and ordering herbs from catalogs, be sure to read carefully the descriptions of recommended conditions and make sure that the plant you want will grow quite happily in your garden.

10 best herbs for shade

angelica   comfrey   elderberry   ginseng   hepatica   Joe Pye weed   lungwort   self-heal   sweet woodruff   white snakeroot

light

The amount of sun that your garden receives should be an important consideration when choosing your herbs. A sunny spot is the preferred homesite of most herbs, including nearly all the popular culinary types. Many will also grow reasonably well in partial shade, as long as they can bask for at least four hours in full sunlight.

If your yard is a shady one, make those on the list (see page 25) the foundation of your garden, but experiment with others, too. Large leaves are often a signal that a plant will grow happily in most shady situations. Try to avoid planting herbs with gray or silvery leaves in full shade however; they usually decline quickly.

soil

Herbs are highly adaptable when it comes to soil type. Soil of average consistency will make most herbs happy, but many grow just as well in either light or dense soils. There's no need to bother with a pH test to check the acidity or alkalinity of your soil, because these easy-going plants will adapt to all but the most extreme conditions. Rich soil encourages fast, loose growth of foliage, which is usually less aromatic than that of herbs grown on a more meager diet.

If you can squeeze a handful of earth into a ball that doesn't crumble immediately when you open your hand, or need a crowbar to break it apart, your herbs will have a suitable home. "Improving"

10 best herbs for dry soils

aloe vera

burdock

cayenne pepper

cilantro

desert tea

fennel

hens-and-chicks

santolina

saw palmetto

yerba mate

herbs for problem soils

HERBS FOR ACID SOILS angelica, elderberry, ginseng, lungwort, senna, sweet woodruff, wild strawberry, witch hazel

HERBS FOR ALKALINE SOILS Austrian briar rose, cucumber, culinary sage, ephedra, salvias, thymes

HERBS FOR HARDPAN OR CALICHE hens-and-chicks, mints, oregano, thymes

the soil is usually not necessary for herbs. If you have extremely dense clay, however, you can add sand, gravel, compost, or other materials to your soil to lighten its texture. Alternatively you can simply select plants to fit your site instead of changing your soil. Herbs with taproots usually do well in clay soil. Because there are so many different herbs to choose from, you're sure to find a number of plants that will thrive in your soil, no matter what its qualities.

Soils that are extremely acid or alkaline, and soils underlaid by an impenetrable rock-hard layer of caliche or hardpan, present special problems for herb gardeners. Either plant varieties that can adapt to these conditions, or make raised beds for your plants. Growing herbs in containers is another way you can expand the possibilities of your herb collection, regardless of the quality of your garden soil.

drainage

How fast water drains through your soil is more important to the health of your herbs than the texture or fertility of your soil. Soil that drains slowly, so that the plant roots are frequently in wet soil, will cause most herbs to go into quick decline. Rapidly draining sand and other light soils are usually not a problem, as long as you plant herbs that don't have a thirsty nature.

Compost is a magic cure-all for drainage problems. It fluffs up dense soils, adding air and allowing moisture to pass through easily. It works similar magic on light soils by retaining water that normally dissolves away too soon. Make or buy your compost, and mix it in using liberal amounts.

Growing herbs in raised beds or pots is one way to solve drainage difficulties. You can also select herbs that are adapted to the moisture conditions of your soil. Angelica, beebalm, and some varieties of hibiscus will flourish in wet sites, while aloe vera, cilantro, and burdock like the dry.

Add generous amounts of gravel to clay soils to increase air spaces and improve drainage

preparing and improving the site

You're almost there—now you've thought about what you want to grow and where, it's time to get the bed ready. Preparing a site for herbs is much the same as for flowers, with extra emphasis on giving soil the fluffy, fast-draining soil texture that new roots love.

making the bed

While herbs are generally hardy, adaptable plants, they still benefit from a helping hand and a little groundwork to welcome their new roots.

REMOVING SOD

Peeling up areas of lawn to make way for herbs is a much faster job than you may expect. Grass roots are so interwoven, they will hold together firmly while you roll up your lawn like an old carpet. Here's how to do it:

1 Use a long-bladed digging tool to lift out any dandelions or other deep-rooted weeds.

2 Slice through the turf with a shovel along one edge of the bed—the shorter side, if you're clearing a rectangular area. If your bed is wider than about 2 feet, work in sections.

3 Push the shovel blade in at an angle beneath the edge to sever and lift the first few inches of grass roots.

4 Working on your knees, use your hands to begin rolling back the grass. Use a trowel to lift any stubborn spots as you peel up the lawn.

5 Continue until the bed is cleared. Put the sod strips on your compost pile, grass side down.

6 Turn the newly bare soil with a shovel, digging at least one blade deep. Chop up any clods using a hoe, then rake smooth.

COMPOST

Rescuing treasure from trash is a heartwarming concept for any frugal gardener. Any material that began its life as a plant is fair game for the compost pile: weeds, hedge trimmings, grass clippings, straw, vegetable scraps from the kitchen, newspapers, paper grocery bags—you get the idea. Pile them all up, keep them moist and aerated, and in a couple of months you can scoop out the crumbly black compost from the bottom of the pile.

Earthworms and a million other organisms, from bacteria to beetles, do the work of decomposition by digesting your raw materials. To keep them well fed, aim for a mix of about one part "green" or fresh plant material to four parts "brown" or dry plant material. In other words, for every bucket of kitchen scraps you toss on the pile, add four buckets of straw or crumpled strips of torn newspaper. Don't worry about getting the proportions exact; just use your eyes and nose to tell you if the mix is working. If you smell a sour odor, add more dry matter; if the pile doesn't seem to be breaking down, add more fresh green stuff. Avoid any meat, grease, or dairy products in the pile, as they will attract pests.

You can build your compost pile within a pen, keep it out of sight in a revolving drum-type container, or just let it grow as a freeform heap. Spray with a hose if rain is scanty so the pile stays moist but not wet.

GRAVEL AND SAND

If your garden soil is heavy, slow-draining clay, a few wheelbarrow loads of gravel or coarse sand will give the roots of your plants better breathing space. Prepare the bed as usual, removing sod and turning the soil. Then dump the sand, gravel, or both, on top of the new bed. Rake it out to a depth of at least 2 inches, then use a hoe to mix it into the top 6 inches of soil, the depth to which most herb roots will grow.

Be sure to buy coarse builders' sand, not fine-grained play sand, because larger grains are more efficient at improving air and water spaces in clay soil.

Turn over the layers of compost to incorporate more oxygen, which hastens decomposition

choosing plants

Start your shopping with a visit to a nursery or garden center, where you can see, touch, and sniff the plants you've read about. Make a list so you remember to buy at least some of the herbs you've planned space for, but enjoy those impulse buys, too.

When you are faced with so many exciting possibilities for your herb garden, bear in mind the time that you will want to spend on weeding and other care. Lean toward the conservative side when buying—it's always better to start small, and you can always add more plants later.

savvy shopping

Examine the plants closely at garden centers and other outlets before you buy. Always choose the healthiest looking specimens—plants with compact growth, strong stems, and no sign of yellowing or other sickliness. If you are ordering through the mail, be sure to read the catalog carefully so that you know what size plants you are getting, and make sure that the plant will be well suited for your climate zone.

If you're on a budget or simply enjoy growing your own plants, turn to the seed rack on your herb quest. For less than the price of a single herb plant, you can grow dozens to fill your garden.

As your garden expands beyond the basics, explore the huge selection of herbs to be found in mail-order catalogs and via the Internet—dozens of cultivars of thyme, thirty kinds of lavender… the offerings can seem endless.

2
planting

Treat the new additions to your herb garden with tender care when you settle them into their new home, and you'll be rewarded with years of use and beauty. Start with young plants, sow seeds, or mix the methods for a lush and bountiful garden.

how to plant your herbs

Herb plants offer instant gratification: you can take them straight home and pop them in the ground. But the cost can mount up quickly. Starting herbs from seed will stretch your budget and give you the pleasure of knowing your herbs from their first sprout.

from the beginning

A few herbs, including popular garlic, are best grown from bulbs. Dill, anise, and other annual herbs, which grow for only a single year, are best grown from seed, sprinkled directly into the prepared garden bed. They sprout fast and zoom to a decent size in a short time, outpacing the weeds that infiltrate the bed.

Growing perennial herbs from seed is wonderfully gratifying, and a big moneysaver if your garden includes more than a few plants of each type. Start perennial herb seeds in pots; the seedlings are tiny at first, and in a garden bed they'd be quickly overshadowed by lusty young weeds. Perennial herbs are slower to sprout than annuals. Most make their appearance in a week or two, but three notorious characters are practically impossible. Leave angelica, lady's mantle, and sweet woodruff to the dedicated experts, and plant parsley seed only if you have a lot of patience: it can take months to sprout.

STARTING FROM SEED

Growing herbs from seed can be an almost year-round project, no matter where you live.

• In mild-winter areas, sow seeds for annual and perennial herbs outdoors all year long.

• In colder zones, sow annual herbs directly into the garden during spring, summer, and fall.

When you come to potting your new herbs, fill containers with a lightweight, fluffy planting mix that will resist compaction from repeated watering, confined space, and a lack of aerating earthworms. Wet the mix before adding plants

indoors In cold-winter climates, especially in late winter, when the cold-weather blahs are at their worst, starting perennial herb seeds indoors allows you to get a jump on the growing season. Sow the seeds about six weeks before you want to move them outdoors. Plant the seeds in pots of soilless seed-starting mix and keep them on a tray on a sunny windowsill or under lights. Be sure to label all the pots so you remember what's what! To water, fill the tray with water and let the roots absorb it from the bottom. Apply a water-soluble, all-purpose plant food about once a week. **outdoors** Sprinkle the seeds of fast-growing annual herbs right where you want them to grow, following the instructions on the packet for an idea of spacing and seed depth. Most annual herbs will sow their own seeds as the season comes to a close, giving you the beginnings of a new crop for next year.

You can start perennial herb seeds in pots outside at any time of the year if you live in warm-winter climates. In colder areas, start

10 best herbs to grow from seeds

anise basil caraway cilantro culinary sage dill German chamomile lavender nasturtium shepherd's purse

Mix very fine seeds with sand to help control the amount you sow. Spray the soil lightly with water and cover with plastic wrap to stop the surface from drying out

WHEN TO PLANT YOUR HERBS

agastache	sow seeds from spring to early summer
basil	sow seeds from spring through midsummer
borage	sow seeds from spring to early summer
burdock	plant roots in spring
chamomile	sow seeds from spring to summer
chicory	sow seeds from spring to midsummer
cucumber	sow seeds in late spring through early summer, after soil is warm
dandelion	sow seeds in early spring
dill	sow seeds from spring to late summer
fennel	sow seeds from spring through early summer
foxglove	sow seeds from spring through early summer for bloom the following year
garlic	plant bulbs in spring or in fall
horseradish	plant roots in spring
hyssop	sow seeds in spring through early summer
Jupiter's beard	sow seeds from spring through early summer for bloom the following year
lavender	sow seeds from spring through early summer for bloom the following year
lemon balm	sow seeds in spring through midsummer
morning glories	sow seeds in spring, after soil is warm
parsley	sow seeds from spring through midsummer
poppies	sow seeds in spring. Sow next year's crop in fall
saffron	plant bulbs (corms) in spring or fall
sweet cicely	sow seeds from spring through midsummer for bloom following year
tansy	sow seeds from spring through early summer for bloom the following year
yarrow	sow seeds from spring to early summer

perennials outside in pots when the weather warms in spring, and continue sowing through the early summer. After sowing the seeds in soil-less potting mix, sprinkle a handful of fine gravel on top to help prevent soil and young plants from being washed away during rain showers. Keep the pots collected together on old cookie sheets. Fertilize them about once a week using water-soluble plant food. When the young herbs are large enough to handle directly and to weed around, transplant them into the garden.

If you are sowing seeds or planting roots and bulbs, the guidelines in the chart (left) will help you to grow them successfully in cold-winter areas. In areas where the winters are milder, you can sow and plant year-round. Potted plants are not included—plant these anytime during the growing season: year-round in mild climates or spring and early fall in cold-winter areas. You can also find instructions relating to particular plants in the herb directory (pages 75–187).

STARTING WITH BULBS OR ROOTS
Horseradish, garlic, saffron, and other herbs that have bulbous or thick, fleshy roots are usually sold as bare bulbs or roots, although you may occasionally find plants that have already been started offered for sale in pots.

Plant bulbs and roots in spring, summer, or early fall in prepared soil at the recommended depth. Mark the spot with a plant label; it may take several weeks for the shoots to emerge.

STARTING WITH PLANTS

Young herb plants are usually sold in small plastic pots. Make a hole in the bed or container with a trowel, then hold the pot upside-down with one hand across the top to catch the plant as it slips out. If it is reluctant to leave the pot, pull gently on the plant until it slides free. Place the rootball in the hole at about the same depth that it was growing in the pot. Fill and firm the soil around it, and water well.

supermarket finds

Shop at the produce counter of your supermarket for economical starts of horseradish and garlic. Look for the gnarled, brown roots of horseradish and the familiar white papery globes of garlic. Store in the refrigerator until you're ready to plant. Separate the garlic cloves and plant individually, about 6 inches apart and 4 inches deep. Plant horseradish roots with the smaller end pointing down, and the top about 2 inches below the surface.

Spring is not just a time for hard work and planting duties, it's also time to enjoy the fresh bursts of floral display your garden will be putting forth

PLANTING CONTAINERS

Containers give you more growing space and serve as focal points in the garden. For the lushest arrangement, fill your windowboxes, clay pots, and other containers with as many plants as you can squeeze in. A grouping of herbs of various habits—vertical, mounded, and sprawling—will make your container garden more interesting. Soften the look a little with edging plants that will trail over the rim.

After filling the container with potting soil to within 2 inches of the rim, arrange the herbs, still in their original pots, until you are pleased with the combination. Since you will be supplying all the nutrients and water they need, you can plant them closer than you would in the garden.

Water thoroughly after planting. Fertilize with a water-soluble, all-purpose plant food about once a week to keep the plants growing vigorously. Depending on the size of the container and the weather, you may need to water your container garden as often as once a day. Wiggle a finger into the soil; if it feels dry, it's time to water. Fill the container to the brim, let it drain, then repeat.

Be generous when planting containers, and snuggle in as many plants as possible. Because you'll be supplying their food and water, they will grow vigorously even in cramped quarters

companion planting

Many gardeners believe that herbs hold the power to deter pests from neighboring plants, and scientific research into some of the claims shows there may be a basis in fact. In any case, it can be fun to conduct your own trials to test the theory in your own backyard.

According to some gardeners, it's the strong scent and flavor of herbs that repels pests before they can attack. In some cases, such as garlic and roses, the action is thought to happen above-ground; in others, the repellent is said to be in the herb's roots, for example, marigolds are believed to deter root nematodes.

At the very least, companion planting is a harmless exercise. At best, you may find that combining aromatic herbs with your favorite

ornamentals does indeed reduce the outbreaks of aphids and other pesky critters. Keep records so that you can calculate whether such occurrences are due to a general cyclical swing in insect populations, and evident throughout the garden, or if they do seem to be direct cause-and-effect.

PROTECTIVE HERBS

herb	companion	reputed benefits
basil	peppers	enhanced growth
basil	tomatoes	improved flavor and growth
borage	strawberries	improved flavor
borage	tomatoes	tomato hornworm repellent; improved flavor
catnip	peppers	aphid repellent
catnip, cilantro, tansy	potatoes	Colorado potato beetle repellent
chives	roses	aphid repellent
cilantro	peppers	aphid repellent
dill	cabbage family crops	improved flavor
garlic	roses	aphid repellent
lettuce	radishes	flea beetle repellent
mints	any	ant repellent
nasturtium	cucumbers	cucumber beetle repellent
rosemary, sage	carrots	carrot rust fly repellent
rue, wormwood	radishes	flea beetle repellent
sage	cabbage family crops	cabbage moth repellent
summer savory	beans	improved flavor
tansy	raspberries	improved growth and better flavor
tansy	squash, pumpkins	squash bug repellent
thyme	lemon verbena	whitefly repellent

attracting beneficial insects

A gardener's best allies against insect pests are other insects—those of a predatory nature, that is. Many species of insects prey upon others, either by devouring them directly, like the praying mantis, or by feeding them to their young. Wasps scour the garden looking for caterpillars to carry off to the nest as a sort of living larder for their offspring. Other wasps lay their eggs on the bodies of caterpillars, upon which the young feed when they have hatched. Ladybug beetles lay their eggs near a colony of feeding aphids so the predatory larvae have a ready-made food source.

These insect allies are known as beneficials. Flowers of dill, fennel, and other herbs attract nectaring adult beneficials, which will linger in your garden to work as pest-destroyers.

A range of neighborly insects benefit gardens by pollinating flowers as they flit between them

10 best herbs for pots

carrot   dill   fennel   garlic   goldenrod   lavender   mints   oregano   thyme   yarrow

tools and equipment

If you already grow flowers and vegetables, you probably have all the equipment needed for working with herbs. A shovel, hoe, fork, secateurs, knife, and trowel are the basic tools for herb gardening. One other must is labels to help you identify your herbs.

a gardener's toolbox

Well-chosen tools made for the job at hand can make your herb planting and maintenance easy and efficient.

SEED STARTING AND PROPAGATION

A convenient place to work is vital for seed-starting projects. To save your back, work at a potting bench, patio table, or kitchen table. A few pieces of simple equipment are all that you need:

• A plastic drop cloth to cover the table and make cleanup a breeze

• New or recycled plastic pots

• Soilless seed-starting mix, a lightweight formula that eliminates the problems of compaction as well as weed seeds in normal garden soil

• A bucket for wetting the plant mix, which will take several minutes to absorb the water

• Plastic wrap for covering the pots, which speeds the germination process

• Labels to jog your memory and inform guests.

miniblind plant labels

Make your own plant labels from a new, cheap plastic miniblind (not a recycled older model, which may contain dangerous toxins). For less than $10, you'll have a lifetime supply of labels. Snip each slat into pieces of appropriate length to mark containers or planting beds. Use an indelible marking pen to write the name, then push it in beside your plant.

DIGGING TOOLS

Making holes is how a garden begins, so invest in high-quality digging tools that will stand up to heavy use. Try out the shovel before you buy, to make sure its weight and heft are suitable to your strength. Smaller gardeners may prefer a short-handled shovel rather than a full-sized handle. Inexpensive trowels are prone to bending and snapping at the neck when put to hard labor in clay or rocky soil. Seek out a trowel with a single-piece blade and handle, made from cast aluminum or other strong metal.

WATERING TOOLS

Herb seeds are often tiny, as are the seedlings that spring from them. A blast of water from the garden hose or even a dousing with a sprinkler can wash seeds far away, or damage delicate roots and stems. Prevent the problem by buying a mist attachment for your hose. This screw-on wand includes a nozzle that breaks the stream of water into a spray of fine, gentle droplets— perfect for seed beds and young herb plantings.

quick connections

Simplify watering chores by buying an inexpensive Y-connector for the faucet, so that you can hook up two hoses at once, or leave one side free for filling buckets. Also pick up a screw-on "shut-off" valve for the faucet, so that you can flick a switch to stop the water instead of turning the handle. Your total investment will come to less than $10. Your total savings in time and convenience will be priceless.

3
maintaining and propagating

Herbs tend to get a lot of attention in the garden, not because they need it—most are trouble-free—but because they're a pleasure to look at, sniff, and sample. The shadow of the gardener is the best "fertilizer" an herb garden can have. Your frequent presence means potential problems will be quickly spotted and solved.

tending your herbs

A daily stroll through your garden can make maintenance a quick, casual, and enjoyable routine, so that your herbs are vigorous, long-lived, and abundant. Take this time to appreciate a moment's calm in the hustle and bustle of daily life.

weed control

These sneaky interlopers compete with other plants for food, water, and a place in the sun. Prevent their stealthy thievery by getting rid of weeds whenever you spot them.

Good nutrition is just as vital for young herbs as it is for young humans. If a young herb must compete with weeds for food and elbow room, it is apt to be weak and bare-limbed instead of thick and bushy. If fine work is not your forte, you can eliminate early weeding by sowing seeds in pots, where weeds are nonexistent, or planting your garden from purchased plants.

WEEDING SEEDLING HERBS
Sorting seedling herbs from weeds can be a challenge, but it is also a satisfying exercise, and a vital part of successful gardening. The first step in weeding a new herb bed is deciding which plants are "keepers." Determining seedling herbs isn't difficult; a packet of seed will yield dozens of plants that look alike, whereas weeds sprout in all shapes and sizes. And even when very young, herbs carry their characteristic scent. When in doubt, rub a baby leaf and sniff your fingers.

Anise, caraway, cilantro, and dill are annual plants that germinate and grow quickly, unlike perennial herbs like chives, which develop at a much slower rate. Sow annuals thickly and you may not have to weed until the plants are a few inches tall, because they can easily compete with fast-growing weeds. For perennial slow-pokes, weed the bed when your herbs are about ¼ inch tall, so that they don't get overshadowed by more vigorous weeds. Allow yourself at least an hour to weed, and make yourself comfortable; this is a job to take slowly, so enjoy a moment's calm in the hustle and bustle of daily life.

WEEDING ESTABLISHED HERBS

Weeding around older herb plants is much easier because the plants are so much bigger. There will also be fewer weeds thanks to the shade mature plants create, which discourages germination. Pull weeds whenever you see them, or eliminate them by using mulch or other tricks described. Use a twisting motion to remove older weeds; it will pull roots free with less effort. For deep-rooted perennial weeds, buy an inexpensive "dandelion digger"—a thin-bladed hand tool to make lifting stubborn roots a simple task.

minimizing weeds

Outsmart weeds by stopping them from sprouting in the first place, or by removing them wholesale with a hoe, should they appear. Avoid self-sowing herbs, whose progeny will spring up by the score, unless you are planting an informal cottage garden. Fast-spreading herbs that spread by roots can also run rampant in a tidy garden, but it's usually a simple matter to peel up unwanted mats of plants. Mint is the exception: once this super-fast spreader infiltrates an area, it is difficult to remove because new plants spring up from every little bit of root left in the ground.

USING MULCH

A layer of mulch (see page 44) is your miraculous ally in the battle against weeds. The material prevents sun from reaching weed seeds, and also physically blocks their emergence. Grass clippings are an excellent mulch for young weeds, because of their fine texture. To get rid of established weeds, use any organic material you have on hand to smother them. If dandelion and other weeds have gone to seed in your grass, avoid using the clippings as mulch to prevent spreading the unwanted seeds.

TOOLS FOR FINE WORK

- Your bare hands are the best tools for this delicate work. Pull out young offending weeds by grasping them between finger and thumb and pulling upward with a gentle tug. You'll soon develop a rapid, repetitive motion as your eye learns to distinguish weed seedlings from herbs.
- The short, narrow blades of manicure scissors maneuver easily into tight spaces between seedling plants, allowing you to snip off dozens of weed seedlings with a single motion. Cut close to the soil surface; most will not regrow.
- Regular-size scissors work well for "teenage" weeds, in that skinny, gawky stage when they're 2 to 4 inches tall and still thin-stemmed. Gather a handful together and snip off close to the soil.

Hand weed when herbs are small, to prevent competition that could stunt their growth. Mulch older plants with grass clippings or leaves to reduce weeding chores

Oregano, beebalm, chamomile, creeping thyme, and other herbs that spread into thick, dense mats are excellent, living weed-blockers.

mulch

Spreading a layer of organic or inorganic material over soil offers a big payoff for a small investment. Half an hour spent applying mulch saves you hours of watering, weeding, and fertilizing, and keeps your herbs healthy and vigorous. For so little effort on your part, mulch does a lot:

• Keeps the soil from drying out due to evaporation, reducing watering needs.

• Insulates the soil and herb roots within it from the extreme heat of the summer sun.

• Prevents heavy rain from splashing mud onto your herb leaves, keeping them clean for harvest.

• Mitigates winter cycles of freezing and thawing, which damage roots by heaving them upward.

• Decomposing materials attract earthworms and other organisms that improve the texture of the soil, keeping it loose and light.

• Organic mulch adds nutrients to the soil as it decomposes, increasing its fertility gradually.

• Discourages weeds from getting a roothold among your herb plants, and makes them easier to pull because of the loose, moist soil.

• Prevents hard rain from washing away soil and exposing the roots of your herbs.

• Helps herbs of borderline hardiness survive cold winters. A deep, loose layer of straw or fallen leaves acts like a cozy down quilt.

10 herbs that self-sow prolifically

borage

caraway

chicory

dandelion

dill

fennel

German chamomile

lemon balm

Queen Anne's lace

sweet cicely

WITH CONTAINERS

A single ounce of garden soil may contain hundreds of weed seeds. Outwit them by keeping your herbs in containers filled with purchased soil mixes that are free from unwanted seeds. Start slow-growing perennial herb seeds in pots, so they are out of weeds' way for the first several months of their life, or grow an entire collection of herbs in large containers.

DENSE PLANTING

Sunlight is the key stimulant for weed seeds waiting in the soil. When other plants block the light, therefore, few weeds will germinate. Plant your herbs thickly, with little or no space between them, and you'll minimize sprouting of weeds.

GRAVEL MULCHES

Gravel is hard working as well as good looking. It confers most of the benefits of organic mulches, except for bolstering soil fertility. It's a good choice for humid areas, as it doesn't decompose. Use a 2-inch layer of small-sized gravel, about the size of a pea or smaller, so that weeds can't get a roothold between large stones. You'll find gravel sold by the bag, ton, or truckload at home supply stores and landscaping services. Don't worry if gravel gets mixed with the soil; it helps drainage.

ORGANIC MULCHES

Readily available, sometimes inexpensive (or often free), organic mulches are the most popular choice for garden beds. Make use of materials from your own yard, like compost or fall leaves that have been chopped into smaller pieces with a lawnmower. Apply a 2-inch-deep layer over the bed and renew as it decomposes. Sheets of newspaper make an efficient mulch; disguise it with a layer of more attractive material. For seedlings, apply a thin layer of fine-textured mulch.

Water-soluble fertilizers and foliar sprays encourage vigorous growth of herb foliage

watering

Truly low-maintenance plants, herbs rarely need supplemental water once established, although large-leaved herbs often need more than those with small or feathery leaves. Herbs with gray or silver foliage are usually the least thirsty. Water small seedlings with a fine mist to avoid dislodging roots. If rain is scarce or your plants show signs of wilting, water established herbs with a stronger stream, or apply water at their roots with a low-care soaker hose or drip irrigation, which will emit water at soil level and prevent moisture from being lost to evaporation. Spray herb foliage the day before harvesting to wash off any dust or debris that has collected.

fertilizing

A lean diet is not a mean diet when it comes to herbs. Nearly all herbs thrive in soil of average to poor fertility, with many growing well in almost pure gravel or sand, or tiny crevices of soil. Nitrogen-rich fertilizers or manure encourage fast, succulent growth of leaves and stems, which dilutes the concentration of oils that give an herb its characteristic fragrance and flavor.

The best fertilizer for herbs is compost, which supplies a slow, steady, long-lasting nutrient boost. Spread a 1–2-inch-deep layer around your herb plants as a springtime mulch; if another mulch is already in place, use a hoe to pull it back so you can apply the compost to bare soil and then replace the mulch. For tips on making your own compost, see page 29.

winter protection

Hardy perennial herbs, plus any seedlings of self-sown herbs that pop up during fall, should survive winter in the garden without any assistance from you. To protect tender herbs, there are many ways to pull out the winter blankets: indoors and out.

transplanting indoors

Moving from garden to kitchen window is a traumatic process for herbs acclimated to the outdoor life. Ease the process by beginning early.

1 Younger, smaller plants adapt more easily to indoor culture than established herbs. Instead of trying to move an entire clump of lemongrass, for instance, slice off a small section with a stout knife or sharp spade. Take divisions or cuttings in late summer, and root them in 4-inch plastic pots of soilless potting mix. If you

want to try bringing in an established plant, prune it back by one-third to one-half in early fall and transplant it into an appropriately sized container.

2 Place the potted herbs in a lightly shaded place, protected from the wind, to mimic the reduced light of the indoor garden.

3 In fall, before the first frost, check your potted herbs for any pests before bringing them indoors. Place them on a bright windowsill or under full-spectrum or fluorescent lights, and keep them away from heat sources that will quickly dry them out. Supply each pot with a saucer to catch drips; water drains fast through soilless potting mix, but the roots will absorb the water from the saucer.

4 Be prepared for your herbs to drop some leaves as they become accustomed to the new conditions. Water whenever the soil is dry to the touch an inch deep.

BOOSTING SURVIVAL OUTDOORS

Get your herb garden fit for the winter season with these preventive maintenance tricks.

• Stop pruning and pinching herbs in early fall, so plants don't produce new growth, which is soft and highly susceptible to winterkill.

• If fall rains are scarce, water the garden generously before the ground freezes.

• Erect windbreaks of burlap or evergreen boughs for herbs that will be exposed to the brunt of prevailing winter winds.

• Move light containers of perennial herbs into a cool or unheated garage for the winter months. Water thoroughly before the soil freezes.

• Snuggle borderline-hardy herbs in a deep layer of straw or loosely piled leaves.

• Lay branches of spruce, fir, or any other dense needled evergreens over borderline-hardy herbs when the ground threatens to freeze.

• Treasure snow cover, which has excellent insulation properties. If snow is light and fluffy, you can even shovel it onto any exposed herb plants.

GROWING UNDER GLASS

Savor garden-fresh herbs year-round by growing them under glass. A greenhouse is ideal for keeping herbs through winter, but a simple cold frame will also let you enjoy that fresh-picked flavor.

Enjoy a nibble of fresh herbs with your Christmas dinner by sheltering selected plants with freeze-proof glass covers. Glass domes called cloches—or an overturned clear glass mixing bowl—will help to keep herb plants snug.

quickie cold frames

Solar heat warms up a glass-topped cold frame to keep parsley, rosemary, thyme, and other herbs fresh and green, even in cold weather. Kits are widely available, or you can construct your own frame from plywood and an old window sash. For an almost-instant cold frame, join four bales of straw into a rectangle and top with a recycled window. Prop the glass top open a few inches on sunny late-winter days to prevent too much heat from building up inside.

pests and diseases

Few insects bother herb plants, perhaps because of the substances that create their strong aromas. In fact, herbs are more likely to be pest repellents than fodder for hungry insects. Disease is also rare, and easily managed by non-chemical means.

organic controls

Non-chemical methods of controlling pests and diseases solve problems while assuring that herb plants are perfectly safe for you to use in cooking, teas, medicines, and other preparations. To maintain a healthy foundation for your herb garden, practice preventive medicine:

a pretty "pest"

You may notice a striking caterpillar on plants of dill, fennel, parsley, carrot, and Queen Anne's lace. Banded with black and yellow, this large green critter is the larval form of the beautiful black swallowtail butterfly. Instead of destroying this garden friend, plant some more of its favorite food plants so there are enough herbs for both of you.

• Keep soil healthy by nourishing the myriad microorganisms it contains with compost and organic mulches.
• Water your plants early in the day so that foliage dries quickly, thus reducing the potential for mildew and other fungal problems.
• In humid climates, prune back herb plants to keep a bit of space around them for improved air circulation. Damp places are breeding grounds for disease organisms.
• Rotate patches of dill and other annual herbs from year to year, so pests don't have a chance to build to problem levels.
• Grow a diverse herb garden. Large areas of a single plant are more inviting to pests.

PROBLEM SOLVING GUIDE

pest or disease	herbs often affected	solution
aphids	caraway, lemon verbena, nasturtium, oregano	snip off infested stems or wipe off aphids with a damp cotton pad
flea beetles	horseradish	lacy, beetle-nibbled leaves are unsightly but harmless to the plant's health. No control is necessary
fusarium wilt	basil	if basil leaves discolor and begin to wilt, pull out affected plants. Plant a new patch with certified disease-free seed in another location
Japanese beetle	basil	in early morning, when beetles are sluggish, tap them into a jar of ammonia
leaf spot	lavender, nasturtium, viola, others	pluck off all leaves showing dark dots and dispose of them in the trash
mildew	beebalm (see left), calendula, cilantro, lemon balm	spray with compost tea made by soaking a shovelful of compost in a bucket of water overnight. Or spray with a mixture of baking soda and water
mint flea beetle	mints	cover plants with floating row covers to prevent damage, which is cosmetically unpleasant but not fatal to the plant
rose chafer	basil	don garden gloves and handpick the beetles, putting them into a jar of ammonia
scale	rosemary	spray with insecticidal soap, or dab a small number of the insects with a cotton swab dipped in alcohol
spider mites	lemon verbena, mints	encourage beneficial insects by growing dill and other rosemary, sage, thyme herbs with clusters of tiny flowers. Spray plants with water, thoroughly spraying both top and undersides of leaves

Blackfly, a common aphid, tends to cluster on the underside of leaves

Sticky growths of scale like to infest the stems of rosemary and tayberry

The rose chafer, here on a globe artichoke flower, often affects basil

propagation

Making more of a good thing is the reason behind propagating your own herbs. Many plants multiply rapidly with a little encouragement from the gardener, giving you an abundance of herbs to extend your plantings, share with friends, or give as gifts.

10 best herbs to propagate from seed

- anise
- basil
- caraway
- cilantro
- coneflower
- dill
- flax
- foxglove
- German chamomile
- lemon balm

seed

Propagating herbs from seed is so simple, you can let your plants do the work for you. All annual herbs produce a generous amount of seeds, many of which will find their way to hospitable soil for next year's crop. If you prefer to direct the process yourself, check the seedheads daily after flowering is finished. When the seeds ripen from green to brown, it's time to collect them.

COLLECTING SEED

You'll need a brown paper grocery bag and a pair of pruners to collect seed, plus shallow trays for separating seed from plant debris. Harvest only one kind of herb seed at a time, so you don't end up with a grab bag of seeds.

1 Determine if the seedhead will release seeds when you shake it: Bend the head over the open bag and tap it firmly. If you hear a pattering of seeds following into the bag, continue harvesting in this fashion.

2 If the seeds are reluctant to fall, snip the entire seedhead and let it drop into the bag.

3 Spread the contents of your bag into a shallow tray, such as a clean, empty pizza box. Dry for about a week to ripen seeds.

4 Rub the seedheads between your fingers to release the seeds. Coneflower seedheads are prickly, however, so wear garden gloves.

5 When all the seedheads are cleaned, shake the box back and forth so that the seeds fall to the bottom.

6 Skim the plant debris off the top with your fingers and pour the remaining seeds into a storage container.

STORAGE AND VIABILITY

Light, heat, and moisture are the enemies of stored seeds. Store your collection in small paper envelopes, zip-top plastic bags, or closed jars in a dark, dry place. Germination rate tends to be high if the seeds are sown during the first year, but will then decrease progressively with age. If your seeds have been stored for longer than a year, sow them that much more thickly to compensate for their lower viability.

division

Imagine making a dozen plants from a single clump of chives, or a hundred new plants of creeping thyme to line a sidewalk. Division is fast and foolproof, and gives you a new generation of good-sized plants within a few short weeks.

Choose herbs with spreading roots to practice on. A shovel works best for slicing thickly interwoven roots and stems with little effort. Sharpen the blade with a whetstone beforehand.

SEPARATING SUCKERS

Young plants that pop up near the parent, and spring from the same root, are called suckers. Shining sumac, white willow, witch hazel, and other shrubby herbs often show this characteristic. Use a shovel to slice young suckers from the main plant, then transplant elsewhere. Water well after replanting, and keep the soil fairly moist until they are growing well on their own roots.

Use a garden fork to dig up a large clump of your herb, and divide by levering two forks apart

Pull each of the divisions into a further two halves. Repeat if the clump still seems to be too large

Make some new planting holes, add compost, and replant the herbs about 1 foot apart. Water well

TIMING

You can divide plants anytime from early spring to midsummer, but the process is easiest in spring, when foliage is just beginning to grow and plants can recover quickly from the operation. To divide plants after they are fully grown, cut back the foliage to about 3–6 inches from the ground before slicing up the parent plant.

Remove suckers during the early spring, when the shrubs are still dormant. The transplants will then have more time to grow a few supporting rootlets before they must nourish a whole new growth of foliage.

TECHNIQUE

1 Water the herb plant the day before, so that the moistened soil will cling to the roots, and thus protect the delicate root hairs, when you lift out the divisions.
2 Keeping the blade of your shovel nearly perpendicular to the ground, slice through the parent plant, removing a section at least 2 inches in diameter—about the size of an herb plant in a starter pot.
3 Continue slicing off pieces from the parent plant until you have gathered as many divisions as you desire.
4 Replant the divisions in prepared soil, and water them generously.

cuttings

Propagating plants by rooting snippets of stem is just as simple as root division, but much less popular, perhaps because it's too tricky to remember which plants will and won't root this way. Lose your hesitation by remembering "Nothing ventured, nothing gained." Try cuttings of any herb you like: if they root, you've gained new plants; if they don't, you've lost only a few minutes' time.

WHEN TO TAKE CUTTINGS

Flexible green stems root faster than tough, woody ones, so clip your cuttings in spring or early summer, when plants are putting out a flush of new growth. This will allow your plants plenty of time to put out strong roots before winter.

HOW TO START CUTTINGS

A patch of reliably moist soil or sand is all that you need to start cuttings. This soil can be in your garden, where you'll have to contend with weeds and remember to water the cuttings, or in a container, where you can easily monitor growth.

Plastic pots 4 inches or larger in size are ideal for rooting cuttings, because they permit the plant to grow a significant amount of roots before transplanting is needed. Group the pots on a tray, where you can water them all at once. A nursery bed dedicated to propagating plants is also a good idea. Mix a liberal amount of compost with the garden soil to lighten the texture so that new roots can easily penetrate and take hold.

TECHNIQUE

1 Examine a healthy, nonflowering stem of the herb you intend to propagate. The bumps from which leaves emerge are called nodes. Using a sharp knife to avoid crushing the stem, slice off a piece about 4–6 inches long, including at least three sets of leaf nodes.

2 Strip the leaves from the bottom 2–3 inches of the stem with your fingers, leaving at least four leaves at the top.

3 If you like, dampen and dip the bare end of the stem into purchased rooting hormone, which will speed the root-growing process.

4 Poke the cutting into the moistened soil of the nursery bed or container, pushing it in so that the bare part is all covered. If the stem is particularly tender, poke a planting hole with a pencil, insert the stem, and firm up the soil around it.

5 Spray the soil with water. Keep very moist but not wet. Cuttings take time to grow roots; keep the soil moist for at least four weeks, until new leaves appear. Thereafter, water often, at least once a week if rainfall is scarce.

Run your thumb and forefinger down the bottom of the stem to remove leaves, but keep a few intact at the top of the stem. Push the cutting into the moist soil of your pot and close the soil gently around it

10 best herbs to propagate from cuttings

artemisia basil beebalm lemon verbena mints rosemary salvias scented geraniums vervain white willow

Strawberries are so cooperative, they send out runners with young plants to do the work of rooting for you. Simply sever the rooted plantlets and transplant elsewhere in the garden

layering

This is a propagation technique for the forgetful-minded! You won't have to remember to water, weed, or mulch plants. This method takes more rooting time, however—it can take as much as a year before herbs are transplanted to the garden. Try it on any herb you like. If it doesn't work, you've lost nothing and gained knowledge.

TECHNIQUE

1 Select a lower stem that is at least moderately flexible. Gently bend it so that it lies flat at ground level.

2 Where the stem reaches the soil, strip the leaves from about a 3-inch-long section of the stem, keeping the leaves at the stem tip intact.

3 Make a shallow nick in the bare stem on the underside, and slice off a ½-inch sliver of covering or bark—the roots will sprout from here. If you wish to speed up the rooting process, dab commercial rooting hormone on the area from which you stripped the bark.

4 Holding the bare stem to the ground with one hand, mound soil over it and pat firmly into place. Secure with a stone or piece of brick.

5 After weeks or months, depending on the plant, roots will form on the buried stem and the leafy tip will be a separate plant, putting out new foliage and branches. To test progress, pull lightly on the stem tip. You'll feel strong resistance if roots are in place. When well rooted, sever it from the parent just before the buried section, and transplant. Water generously for the first few weeks.

10 best herbs to propagate by layering

artemisias · beebalm · culinary sage · elderberry · lemon verbena · rosemary · salvias · strawberry · vervain · white willow

4

harvesting, storing, and using herbs

Once your plantings are flourishing, you can start to experiment with one of the best parts of having a passion for herbs—making use of them. All herbs are, or have been at some point, employed toward human ends, whether curing pesky warts, adding a dash of flavor to mash, or banishing a musty, lived-in smell. This chapter is designed to give you all the preparatory knowledge you need to liven up your life with a little herb magic.

useful parts

Herbs hold their powers in various parts of their structure. Over the centuries, knowledge of which pieces of each plant are best to use for which purposes has been passed along from generation to generation, as well as from culture to culture.

Foliage is the most commonly used part of an herb, but other pieces of an herb plant may also come into play. Leaves, stems, roots, flowers, seeds, bark, and oil—all can be employed, but be sure to pay attention to those parts recommended for use; a tea made from roots instead of leaves, for example, may give unfortunate results.

The method by which the plant parts are prepared is also vital to their use. Some are eaten raw, others boiled or steeped or crushed. Crushed seeds or bark, for example, yield concentrated oils, used for preparations of fennel and some other herbs. You'll find more details on herbal preparations throughout this chapter.

harvesting

Making use of your herbs is an exciting time, whether you're planning to simmer a pot of fresh mint tea or simply to add the color of some calendula petals to an everyday dinner. You can harvest your herbs whenever you feel that inspiration to liven your home and life with flavor, color, or handmade decorations.

If you need any further encouragement, there is also the fact that the more often you pick, the better your herbs will grow. Cutting herbs causes the remaining stems to push out new branches and leaves, resulting in a vigorous, compact plant ready for further harvest.

COLLECTING LEAVES AND STEMS

Foliage and the stems that it grows on are the parts of your herbs you'll be gathering most often—whether you want a sprig of rosemary for roasted potatoes, a basket of basil for summertime pesto, or a bouquet of artemisia for future dried flower arrangements. Collect your harvest in whatever container will comfortably hold your treasure. Your bare hand, or a small basket, is fine to carry a meal's worth of seasonings indoors, but if you're picking mint to serve drinks for a family picnic, take a bigger basket out with you. Take care to wash any leaves sprayed with pesticides.

Snip the tender stems of chives, thyme, dill, and other slender herbs with scissors. Pruners will work better for tough customers like mints, oregano or woody herbs.

when to pick When inspiration strikes, you can harvest your herbs immediately and put them straight to use. If you're planning to store herb foliage, gather it at its most aromatic peak: ideally in mid- to late morning of an overcast summer day, when essential oils are at high levels.

Dry weather generally brings herbs to the height of their aromatic best. After a period of rainy days, the foliage often has a milder scent. In

TIMING THE HARVEST

Gathering herbs is not an exact science. Although flavors and scent vary in strength depending on the season and the weather, you'll still get plenty of your herbs' trademark aromas no matter when you pick.

herb	time to pick	how to pick
annual herbs, including anise, caraway, cilantro, dill	anytime, as needed; for large quantities, cut twice a season, before flowering	cut entire plant to 6 inches from ground; it will regrow for a second cutting. Snip small amounts anytime
basil	repeated cuttings, summer through fall	cut back each stem until plant is about one-third its size. For last cutting, cut entire plant to ground and use the nonwoody stems and all leaves
beebalm	repeated harvests anytime, preferably before flowering	cut back halfway or to ground level
borage	anytime when young	snip flowers when blooms are fresh; pick leaves
culinary sage	anytime, including after frost, when flavor intensifies	cut tender stems. Avoid cutting into woody part of the plant
garlic	late summer to fall	dig bulbs at end of growing season
horseradish	fall	dig root
mints	repeated harvests anytime, preferably before flowering	cut back halfway or to ground level
oregano	anytime, including winter	shear off as much as desired
parsley	anytime, including winter	snip off as much as about half the plant
rosemary	anytime, including winter	snip tender stems. Avoid cutting into woody part of plant
thyme	anytime, including winter	shear off as much as desired

spring, when the foliage is not yet mature, the flavors are usually less powerful. Energy that is diverted to flowers and seed production can also weaken the aroma and flavor of the foliage, so unless you're cutting flowers, harvest your herbs before buds begin to open. In late summer and fall, herbs may begin to look ragged and insect damage may deface the leaves, but this doesn't mean they're not still tasty!

If you get a hankering for herbs from the garden, head outside and snip away no matter what the calendar says. As long as you can find some greenery to snip, you'll enjoy at least a hint of flavor. To avoid stressing the plant, stop snipping perennial herbs from early fall through the onset of winter, so as not to encourage resource-sapping new growth at a time when the plant should be slowing down for the colder months.

HARVESTING SEED

Sweet, licorice-flavored anise seeds, savory caraway, sprightly dill, and other herbs grown for their seeds are harvested for table use just as they would be picked for sowing a later crop—after they have ripened on the plant from soft green capsules to mature brown seeds holding peak flavor inside.

Monitor your flowering herbs to gauge the ripeness of the seeds, so that the seedheads don't scatter the precious cargo before you have a chance to collect them. To harvest the seeds, shake your seedheads into a paper sack. Pour the collection into a cookie sheet or other shallow tray so that you can blow gently across them to remove bits of plant debris before storing.

DIGGING ROOTS

The fleshy roots of burdock, chicory, horseradish, and angelica and the plump bulbs of garlic are storage organs that hold the collected nutrition of a season's worth of photosynthesis. The plant will draw on this stored food the following year, when new growth begins. Understanding this cycle makes it easy to see that the time to dig herb roots is at the end of the growing season, in fall. Dig deep with a shovel to lift the roots from the soil. If your horseradish patch is a large one,

there's no need to uproot the entire thing; just take the roots you need. Shake off any excess soil and wash the roots thoroughly before storing them in the vegetable bin of your refrigerator or drying for later use.

preparing and storing herbs for use

Using herbs fresh is simplest, but you'll also want to put aside a supply of herbs for times when your favorites aren't available. In long-ago times, air drying was the main technique to preserve herbs. Bunches hung to dry still add a quaint touch to the kitchen, but today we can also call upon the microwave, refrigerator, and freezer to prepare herbs for storage. You'll find specific tips for each plant in the herb directory (see pages 75–187).

FRESH USE

A quick spritz with cold water to wash off any dust, and your herbs are ready to add some pizzazz to the family meals or some fragrance to the bath. For culinary use, you'll also want to remove any tough stems that got into the basket. Mince the leaves or use whole, depending on the herb.

DRYING

The faster herbs dry, the more aromatic they will be. Choose your method according to how much time you want to invest. For herbs used in dried arrangements, air drying is best because it preserves the natural form of each stem.

• Old-fashioned air drying, with herbs hung in loose bunches or scattered on screened trays, is the slowest method of drying herbs; it may take weeks for the moisture to fully evaporate.

10 best herbs for drying

burdock root

chicory root

dill

French tarragon

ginseng root

marjoram

oregano

rosemary

sage

thyme

USEFUL PARTS OF FAMILIAR HERBS

herb	part	use
anise	seed	culinary, medicinal
blazing star	root	medicinal
burdock	root	medicinal
calendula	flowers	culinary, medicinal
cardamom	seeds	culinary, medicinal
carrot	root, seeds	medicinal
cucumber	fruit	medicinal
elderberry	flowers, fruit	culinary
elderberry	flowers, fruit bark, root, leaves	medicinal
evening primrose	leaves	medicinal
Joe Pye weed	flowers, leaves	medicinal
Joe Pye weed	root	aphrodisiac
oregano	leaves and stems	culinary
thyme	leaves and stems	culinary
willow	bark	medicinal
willow	catkins	anti-aphrodisiac
witch hazel	bark, leaves	medicinal

don't even need to chop the herbs before freezing; packed loosely, they will crumble easily in your hand when it's time to add them to a cooking pot. Be sure to label the bag so you can quickly identify it later. You can also freeze chopped herbs as ice cubes: Fill each compartment almost to the top with chives or other chopped herbs, top off with water, and freeze. Drop the herb-filled cubes into soups, stews, and other dishes.

OILS AND VINEGARS

Combining herbs and oil creates a flavorful additive for pastas, salads, and other dishes—or indeed, for softening skin. Use an extra-light olive oil as the base for both culinary and cosmetic magic, or try almond oil with sweetly perfumed herbs to flavor desserts. Herb-flavored vinegars add a savory touch in marinades, salad dressings, and sauces. You'll find intriguing recipes in the herb directory, or experiment on your own by beginning with these basic recipes:

• The microwave swiftly speeds up the process, but it requires constant monitoring and frequent reshuffling to dry large quantities (see box).

• A warm oven, set at about 200°F with the door left ajar, is an efficient middle ground, allowing you to process a lot of herbs at one time with minimal fussing. Check your herbs every half hour.

FREEZING

Freezing preserves more of a herb's fresh flavor than drying, and it's even easier to do. Buy a box of resealable freezer storage bags, and you can store enough herbs for a whole winter of use. You

microwave shortcuts

Dried herbs are yours in a flash with a microwave. Ovens vary in power just as herbs do in size and thickness, so experiment with the time you zap each type. Spread herbs of a single kind on a sheet of microwavable paper towels. Try 30 seconds on medium power and then adjust as necessary. Aim to dry them fully, but not to the point of brittleness.

SAVORY HERB OIL

   4 tbsp fresh, chopped herbs, either all one kind
     or in combination
   2 cups light oil, such as olive or sunflower

Crush herbs with a rolling pin or in a pestle. Scrape into a bowl and add 2 tbsp oil, stirring to coat well. Add the rest of the oil, and stir well. Pour into a jar with screw-top lid. Keep at room temperature for two weeks. Strain the oil into a bottle with a screw-on top, or pretty jar if a gift. Add a sprig of herb for a decorative touch. Label, if you like, and store in the refrigerator.

variation For a sweet herb oil to use with fruits or puddings, use almond oil with chopped leaves of scented geraniums, lavender, or rose petals.

HERB VINEGAR

   2 cups white wine vinegar
   4 sprigs of culinary herbs, sized to fit bottle
   OR
   2 tbsp herb seed such as dill, fennel, coriander

Pour vinegar from its original bottle into a fancy bottle, to about 3 inches from top. Poke in herb sprigs or pour in seeds. Cap the bottle. Keep at room temperature for two weeks, then extract herb sprigs or seeds and replace with fresh ones for stronger flavor. Store in refrigerator.

10 best herbs for freezing

basil   chives   dill   fennel   lovage   parsley   peppermint   spearmint   tarragon   thyme

putting herbs to use

Herbs were first pressed into culinary use not to enliven the taste of foods, but to disguise it. Before refrigeration, meat was often more than a little "off" by the time it reached the table, and strong-smelling herbs went a long way toward making it palatable.

culinary magic

Today we use herbs with a lighter hand, enjoying the zing of flavor they bring to favorite dishes. Chicken baked with garlic, for instance, is a savory dish, while chicken with lemongrass smells equally delicious but has a more sprightly taste. Traditional culinary marriages, like sage with turkey stuffing, oregano in tomato sauces, and dill in cucumber salads, have been joined by more adventurous unions. Depend on strong-scented herbs such as garlic, oregano, or sage

when you're cooking "heavier" foods, such as meats, soups, stews, and tomato-based dishes—meals that require a longer cooking time, under which herbs of a less assertive nature might lose their flavor. For foods cooked quickly, such as eggs, potatoes, rice, stir fries, or tofu, try any herb that appeals to you. Salads, cream-cheese spreads, fruit soups, and other dishes that need no cooking showcase the full flavor of any herbs.

TEAS

Herbal teas are a guilt-free pleasure. They have no caffeine or tannin, taste delicious, and carry no calories. The ritual of tea-making itself and the time spent savoring the drink create a little oasis of calm you can indulge in anytime.

Fragrant herbal teas are so easy to make from the garden that you may never need to buy another box. A small bed of chamomile or peppermint gives enough flavor for a whole season's sipping, whether you opt for a steaming cup on a winter night or a chilled glass in summer.

You can make teas from fresh herbs at a moment's notice, or preserve the harvest for later use. Single-flavor teas are delicious, but it's also gratifying to brew your own custom blends. A base of citrusy beebalm tea, for instance, benefits from the extra tang of lemongrass or rosehips. Or enjoy the unexpected hint of licorice with a touch of sweet cicely in the mix.

Soothing effects, both mental and physical, are an added bonus, thanks to herbs' medicinal properties. Try peppermint to calm a queasy tummy, or unwind with a cup of chamomile after a busy day. Teas from the garden are also great as gifts, costing only a few minutes' time, and garnering you with bragging rights in the bargain.

MATCHING FOODS WITH HERBS

food	complementary herb
beans	summer savory, thyme
beef	garlic, horseradish, marjoram, oregano, rosemary, winter savory
biscuits, rolls	dill, fennel, marjoram, oregano, sage, thyme
butter	chives, French tarragon, garlic
butter cookies	anise, caraway
cakes	anise, caraway, cardamom, lavender, lemon balm, lemon verbena, scented geraniums, sweet cicely
chicken and other poultry	cilantro, French tarragon, garlic, lemongrass, lemon verbena, marjoram, mint, oregano, rosemary, sage
coffee	cardamom, chicory
cream cheese	dill, nasturtium, shepherd's purse, watercress
eggs, scrambled	chives, dill, cayenne pepper, French tarragon, lovage, marjoram, oregano, nasturtium, summer savory
fish, crab, or other seafood	anise, basil, chervil, cilantro, dill, French tarragon, lemon balm, lovage, mint, parsley, rosemary, saffron, summer savory, sweet cicely, thyme
hummus	sumac
pancakes	anise, chives, sweet cicely
potato salad	chives, dill, parsley, horseradish, nasturtium, peppergrass, sumac, watercress
potatoes, boiled	horseradish, mint, parsley
potatoes, mashed	chives, garlic
potatoes, oven-roasted	rosemary, thyme
rice	cardamom, cilantro, parsley, saffron
salad, green	borage, chervil, dandelion, fennel, lovage, nasturtium, perilla, shepherd's purse, watercress
sandwiches, meat or cheese	cilantro, horseradish, rosemary
soups, fruit	hyssop, lavender, lemon balm, lemon verbena, sweet cicely
soups and stews	cayenne pepper, chives, garlic, fennel, hyssop, lovage, marjoram, oregano, parsley, peppergrass, summer savory
tofu	lemongrass, rosemary, sage, summer savory
tomato sauce	basil, garlic, marjoram, oregano, parsley, rosemary
vanilla ice cream	lemon balm, lemon verbena, spearmint

beebalm

elderflower

fennel

German chamomile

hibiscus

lemon balm

lemongrass

lemon verbena

mints

rosehip

two ways to brew herbal teas Use a generous teaspoon of dried herbs for each cup of tea. If you're making a larger quantity, figure 1 teaspoon per cup, plus "a spoon for the pot"—an old saying that gives a slightly richer flavor to steeped brews. For fresh herbs, which are less concentrated in flavor than dried, you'll need 2 to 3 tablespoons per cup. Taste the tea after steeping and add honey or other sweetener if you wish.

RECIPE FOR ONE STEAMING CUP

1 Measure a small amount of water into a kettle and bring it to the boil.
2 Measure dried herbs into a tea ball or home-filled teabag.
3 Fill your cup with boiling water, drop in the container of tea, and steep for about 5 minutes.

tea in a teapot Use this method to make a larger amount of hot tea. Measure enough water for several servings into a kettle and bring it to the boil. Meanwhile, measure your chosen herbs into a teapot and press them against the side with the back of a spoon, which will release their fragrant oils. Add boiling water and let the tea steep for about 5 minutes. Pour and enjoy!

ICED TEA BY THE QUART

1 Fill a large saucepan or deep skillet with water and set over medium-high heat.
2 Meanwhile, coarsely chop a generous handful of mint or other fresh herbs, stems and all.
3 Add the herbs to the pan and simmer on a medium heat until you can smell the delicate flavors of the brew. This should take about 5 to 7 minutes.
4 Strain the liquid into a heatproof container. Discard the herbs.
5 Set the tea aside to cool slightly, or add ice to speed the process. This will protect your serving glasses from damage.
6 Fill tall glasses with ice and pour in your custom-made iced tea. Serve it with pride.

EDIBLE GARNISHES

You'll be surprised how much a few green leaves can liven up the appearance of your casseroles or dessert plates. Dress up an everyday platter of pasta with a small bouquet of fresh basil and oregano and your dinner table will instantly be on on the way to that Gourmet Chef look. Nothing but canteloupe for dessert? Make plain melon fancy with a sprig of mint (and maybe a scoop of vanilla ice cream) on the dessert plate.

DON'T GET BUGGED

Insects love the sweet nectar hidden inside herb flowers, but you'll want to be sure not to invite any bugs to dinner. It's easy to pick them from open-faced flowers, but to be sure your edible blossoms are bug-free, treat the insects to a cold chill.

1 Put a few blossoms into a zip-top plastic bag. Seal, without pressing out the air.
2 Set the somewhat inflated bag upright in the refrigerator for about an hour.
3 Insects will flee the flowers to escape the cold, or fall out when chilled. They will come to rest on the sides or bottom of the bag.
4 After about an hour, carefully remove the blossoms, one at a time, and give them a vigorous final shake, upside down, to dislodge any lingering guests.

Whole fresh leaves, colorful blossoms, or even a sprinkling of seeds give meals a finishing touch that makes them look more tempting. All culinary herbs make good garnishes. Select unblemished leaves and flowers. Rinse leaves lightly, but do not wet flowers because their petals may discolor or stick together. Add garnishes just before serving.

• Make herbs of more delicate flavors your first choice, because the idea of a garnish is to complement a food's flavor as well as add eye appeal. A few sprigs of chive blossoms make an oniony accompaniment atop potato salad, more suitable than, say, a spray of licorice-flavored fennel, which would overpower the potatoes.

• Choose your garnish according to the flavor of the food. Any herb you use in the cooking will make a palate-pleasing edible garnish. In Italian dishes, for instance, a sprig of basil or oregano will repeat flavors found in the sauce.

• With herbs of medium to large leaves, such as mint or basil, use a snippet of just a few leaves.

• With thyme and other small-leaved herbs, use a bigger sprig or small bouquet so that the garnish stands out visually on the plate.

EDIBLE FLOWERS

Herb flowers bring bright color to the dinner plate, whether you snip the petals into confetti or use the blossoms whole. Be absolutely sure of your identification before you serve flowers; although the flowers listed here are safe, other garden flowers may cause ill effects when eaten.

10 best herbs for edible flowers

beebalm borage calendula chives garlic nasturtium pansies peppergrass roses violets

medicinal use

Before the days of modern Western medicine, herbs were used as the cure-all for human health needs, from toothache to nervous conditions, snakebite to childbirth. Ages before Viagra appeared, artichokes and coriander were a man's best friends. And not too many years ago, a dose of chamomile tea, not Ritalin, was the prescription for high-strung children.

Plants have been tested for medical use probably as long as humans have shared the planet. Native Americans chewed willow bark to cure their headaches; today we buy bottles of white tablets—aspirin—containing a synthesized version of the willow's salicylic acid. Soothing teas, invigorating soaks, healing poultices—herbs were the key, whether homegrown or sought from a herbal practitioner. In recent years, herbs have gained great popularity, with medical science working feverishly to test the efficiency of these out-of-the-garden or over-the-counter cures.

The reputed curative powers of herbs are fascinating to learn about, but approach their use with caution. Never rely on an old herbal to treat a medical problem. Experimentation can be fatal. The medicinal strength of herbs varies, depending on weather, climate, and soil, so dosage is more guesswork than science. Herbs are powerful plants; monitor yourself for headaches, dizziness, nausea, or other side effects. Do not use them daily for long periods, and do not experiment with medicinal herbs if you are pregnant. It is also important that you tell your doctor about any herbal treatments you are taking when you visit for other ailments.

Today some of the same plants once freely dispensed as curatives are known to be poisons. Other herbs have lived up to their folklore reputations when put under the microscope of science. Digitalis, for example, which comes from the foxglove plant, is still the drug of choice for treating certain heart conditions—as it has been used for more than 200 years.

PROVEN TREATMENTS

Under the hard eye of researchers conducting controlled testing, some herbs have been determined to be effective and accepted medical treatments. No one would dispute the efficacy of

While foxglove (right) is too potent to experiment with medicinally, aloe vera (far right) can be made into a safe and extremely effective ointment, or its thick sap can be used straight from the garden to help heal burns and aches

digitalis or aspirin. Aloe is also widely recognized for its skin-healing properties. Still, many herbs have leaped in popularity thanks only to word of mouth rather than formal scientific research.

The market for herbal treatments has expanded so rapidly in America that science is hurrying to catch up. While researchers set up tests, consumers are gobbling commercially packaged herbal remedies, currently available without prescription. Clinical trials are under way to test the efficacy of many popular herbal remedies, including echinacea for allergies, St. John's wort for depression, saw palmetto for prostate problems, and ginkgo biloba for memory loss. While other countries have reached positive conclusions about these plants, the jury of American science is still out on their overall effectiveness.

SAFE HERBS FOR COMMON COMPLAINTS

health problem	herb
aching joints	chervil, coriander, thyme
antibacterial, antiseptic	calendula, lavender, lovage, marjoram, oregano, peppermint
bad breath	anise, mint, parsley, sweet cicely
broken heart	viola ('heartsease')
constipation	dandelion, fennel
flatulence	beebalm, caraway, coriander, ginger, lemon balm, lovage, peppermint, summer savory
frazzled nerves	chamomile, dill, goldenrod, lavender, lemon balm
hangover	thyme
hiccups	dill
insect stings	aloe, goldenrod, hens-and-chicks, summer savory
insomnia	chamomile, dill
nasal and sinus congestion	horseradish, sage, violet
stomachache, indigestion	dill, fennel, lovage, peppermint
warts	calendula, dandelion

A little dab'll do you when it comes to taking herbal medicines: one single teaspoonful is a common dosage

glossary of medicinal preparations

INFUSION add herbs to boiling water, cover, and steep for about 10 minutes.

DECOCTION boil hard plant parts (seeds, bark, roots) in water for about 10 minutes; steep for 15 to 20 minutes; strain and use.

TINCTURE mix herb with alcohol and add water to reach a 50% alcohol solution; let stand for two weeks, shaking daily, before straining for use.

POULTICE mix dried or fresh herbs with a warm, wet, gluey flour-and-water mixture and apply to skin; wrap with cloth to hold in heat and moisture.

COMPRESS soak a cloth in hot infusion or decoction, wring out, and apply.

Warnings have been issued for the once-popular herbal treatment, ephedra, which tests show can cause stroke, heart attack, and other side effects.

PROMISING POTENTIAL

In recent years, more and more plants have gone into the laboratory as scientists experiment with unlocking their medicinal secrets. Collectors scour the world, searching out new plants to be examined for medically valuable compounds, and collecting any passed-down folklore remedies that can be tested for their use in modern culture.

Evening primrose is one of those remarkable recent discoveries. Its oil contains gamma-linolenic acid (or GLA), which studies in Great Britain and elsewhere have shown to be effective for treating such disparate conditions as eczema, premenstrual syndrome, and even alcoholic hangovers. It has shown promise in more dramatic areas as well: obesity, multiple sclerosis, and arthritis.

Madagascar periwinkle is another potential miracle herb, which may be effective in combating cancer. Because American medicine requires extensive testing to assure efficacy and safety, the time between a trumpeted discovery and its widespread use may form years or even decades. Other herbal cures are likely to be on the horizon shortly, as more and more attention is focused on these age-old helpers of humanity.

home decor

Decorating trends come and go, but there's always a place for herbs in the home. Whether you weave them into wreaths or set them about as potpourri, herbs offer the same benefits indoors as they do in the garden and kitchen: they look pretty, they smell good, and they have a soothing effect. Putting your own plants to use in home decoration makes your living space feel more personal, and gives you that wonderful feeling of, "I made it myself!"

DECORATIVE ARRANGEMENTS

A wire wreath or swag form, a spool of florists' wire, and an hour or two of time are all it takes to make a beautiful, long-lasting arrangement from homegrown herbs. Try a wreath of culinary herbs for the kitchen wall, or add a lavender circlet to the bathroom for a natural air freshener. Dried bouquets are even easier: just insert stems of dried herbs into a block of floral foam hidden inside a basket, vase, or other attractive container. Or fill a small vase or glass jar with a simple handful of lavender blossoms on bare stems, dressed up with a raffia or ribbon bow. All the supplies you'll need for herbal home crafts are widely available and reasonably priced at craft and hobby shops and discount stores.

It takes a surprising amount of herbs to make a lush-looking arrangement: about 15 fist-sized bunches for a 10-inch-diameter wreath, for example. Prepare the herbs by hanging them upside-down in loose bunches to air dry, as described on page 59. If you're more the instant-gratification type, you can also make decorative arrangements with freshly picked herbs and let them dry in place. Because the stems are likely to bend downward as they dry on the form, monitor your arrangement so you can tuck any strays back into position.

Choose a combination of herbs that pleases your eye. Soft greens and grays can be completely satisfying, or you may want to punch up the arrangement with the deep red of perilla or 'Purple Ruffles' basil, or include a dash of color from dried blossoms of beebalm, tansy, safflower, calendula, or roses.

10 best herbs for dried arrangements

artemisias

beebalm blossoms

chive blossoms

lavender

perilla

rosemary

safflower blossoms

sage

santolina

thyme

MAKING AN HERB WREATH

1 Measure the circumference of the wreath form in inches and divide by four to estimate how many bunches of herbs you will need. (This allows for overlapping herbs so that 4 inches of foliage is visible from each bunch.)

2 Trim the stems of each bunch to a uniform length, about 6 inches, with pruners.

3 Lay out a trial circle on your work surface, placing each bunch on top of the stems of the preceding bunch. Rearrange them until you are happy with the combination.

4 Wire the first bunch securely to the wreath form with florists' wire. Cut with tin snips and bend the loose end inside the stems.

5 Lay the next bunch of herbs over the stems of the preceding bunch. Wire the stems of the second bunch into place.

6 Proceed in the same direction with the next bunch, and repeat until the form is filled.

7 To cover the stems of the last bunch on the form, insert the stems of a final bunch under the foliage of the first bunch. Wire into place.

8 Hang the wreath and admire your handiwork.

POTPOURRI

It's mystifying how a French word that translates to "rotten pot" ever came to describe the collection of aromatic materials we think of today as potpourri. Language difficulties aside, an herbal potpourri adds a gentle scent that freshens indoor rooms with natural odors of beebalm, chamomile, lavender, lemon verbena, rosemary, roses, scented geraniums, or thymes. With a gar-

Mix spices and essential oils with your flowers, add orris root to make the scent last longer, and store in an airtight jar

denful of fresh herbs to choose from, you can blend clean-scented lemon mixtures for the kitchen, romantic lavender fragrances for bed or bath, invigorating rosemary for the office, or a host of other possibilities for every room.

Keep your herbal potpourri in a small bowl. Stir the mixture occasionally to release more scent and bring fresher material to the top. Commercial potpourris depend on scented oils that may be artificial or natural in origin. For a longer-lasting and stronger effect, you can add natural oils of lavender, lemon, or other fragrances, available at craft stores, to your mixtures, or let the herbs alone perfume your air with a more delicate touch. Orrisroot, a common fixative, helps herbal potpourris last longer too, but with an herb garden at your disposal, you may choose to forgo the fix and replenish with fresh material as often as you see fit. Dry your herbs for potpourri using any method covered on page 59–60.

HOW TO MAKE POTPOURRI

1 Strip leaves from selected dried herbs by running thumb and forefinger down the stem. Separate flowers into small florets or petals, depending on size. Discard the stems.
2 Fill container with your herb blend and stir to combine.
3 Drizzle with essential oil and/or fixative if desired. Stir again.
4 Place the bowl on a shelf or table near traffic paths in the house, so passersby can enjoy it.

CANDLES

Herb leaves and flowers offer appealing shape and color to the outer surfaces of candles. A simple arrangement is best, so that the scalloped leaf edges, delicate stems, or tiny leaves can be best appreciated. Look for candle-making wax, wicks, and molds at craft and hobby shops. Follow the package directions to melt the wax. Before filling the mold with wax, position the herbal decorations. If you like a slightly obscured look, with the herbs peeping through a thin film of wax, pour melted wax into the mold and tilt to coat the sides. Carefully press each leaf or flower into the soft wax. If you prefer the leaves or flowers to be more visible, use tiny dabs of melted wax to anchor each one in place before pouring in the rest of the wax.

NOTECARDS AND PAPER

Specialty papers with petals or leaves pressed into the sheets are pricey but beautiful. Create similar handmade paper yourself.

Fill a blender with crumpled strips of paper, add a cup of water, and blend to a soupy liquid. Add more paper, and repeat. Stir in a cup of your chosen plant parts. Pour the slurry onto a framed window screen, and squeegee it into a thin layer. Allow to dry in the sun to slight dampness, then carefully peel the paper off the screen. Flatten the paper using an iron set on medium-high heat, then cut into pieces sized to fit notecard envelopes. Fold, and iron the crease, if desired.

Herbs enliven candles by releasing scent at their base, adding decoration to the wax, or providing a delicious scent through extracted essential oils

10 best scented herbs for cosmetic use

bee balm

chamomile

German
chamomile

lavender

lemon balm

lemon verbena

rosemary

roses

scented
geraniums

thyme

cosmetic preparations

Your herb garden is a patch of perfumes, just waiting to be used to scent your clothes, skin, and hair. While smell alone is enough to calm the senses, herbs can also add shine to your tresses, smooth rough skin, help fight germs with natural antibacterial properties—and, according to some herbal lore, may even stop baldness in its tracks. Using your herbs in homemade cosmetics offers yet another great gift from the garden for birthdays and special occasions.

LOTIONS

Among the easiest cosmetics to cook up at home, skin lotions are simple to make using an inexpensive, unscented store-bought hand lotion. Buy an economy-size bottle to mix with scented herbs and decant into smaller, more decorative containers that you find in craft stores, catalogs, or recycle from your own store of bottles.

You can also make water-based herbal lotions to use as astringents, to help clear up skin problems. Calendula is particularly effective for this use. To help dry up pimples, fill a cup of calendula flowers with boiling water, cover, and steep for 20 minutes. Allow to cool, then splash onto the face.

SOAPS AND SHAMPOOS

Check craft stores for soap-making supplies, and substitute your own herbs for the oils or scents supplied by commercial makers. Rosemary is an excellent choice for hand soap, because its small, stiff leaves provide a bit of abrasive cleaning power and release a sharp, piney scent as you scrub. Lemon-scented thyme and other lemony herbs are ideal for all-purpose shower soaps.

Although you can actually make a lathery shampoo from the herb called soapwort, hair rinses for after shampooing are a better way to take advantage of your favorite herb scents, because you don't rinse them out. Simmer a big handful of lavender, lemon balm, beebalm, chamomile, or other favorites in boiling water for about 15 minutes. Strain and cool, and your hair rinse is ready to use. Just pour through your hair after shampooing, then dry and style as usual.

SCENT

Perfume makers use specialized equipment to press the scented oils from herbs, a job that's beyond the reach of home gardeners. But you can

---

LAVENDER LOTION

1 Use about 2 tablespoons of dry lavender for each cup of lotion. Bruise the lavender in a mortar or with a spoon, to release as much oil as possible.
2 Using a funnel, pour the lavender into the bottle of lotion. Recap and shake well.
3 Shake daily for about two weeks.
4 Allow the bottle to sit undisturbed for several days, so the herbs can settle to the bottom.
5 Stretch a piece of cheesecloth over a funnel and secure with a rubber band.
6 Pour lotion from original bottle into smaller containers. The cheesecloth will trap the pieces of lavender, which would be irritating when the lotion is applied.

Indulge yourself by concocting your own lotions, soaps, and scents direct from the garden—a sensory treat commercial brands just can't match!

still take advantage of the delightful aromas of lavender, thyme, and other herbs to add sensory delight to your bath and bed.

For instant relaxation therapy after a stressful day, gather a handful of lavender, chamomile, beebalm, or other scented favorites from your herb garden, tie the stems with string and hang from the faucet of your bathtub. As you draw your bath, the forceful stream of water will bruise the herbs, releasing their heady scent into the tub and steam. Settle back and indulge!

Make your bed a sensory haven by slipping sprigs of lavender, lemon verbena, rose-scented geranium, or whatever herb most delights your nose, between the linens on the shelf. Or tuck a stem of lemon balm or other pleasant-smelling herb directly inside your pillowcase near to the top seam, where the gentle scent will best permeate your sweet dreams.

Pile a loose handful of dried scented herbs in the center of a white man's handkerchief, collect the corners at the center, and secure the bundle with a rubber band or tie for a fast and easy sachet to tuck into your drawer of dainty under-things or among your silk scarves. For a fancier sachet, which is suitable for gift-giving, use a square of pretty cotton fabric and fasten it together with a ribbon.

herbs that encourage wildlife

One of the best side effects of planting herbs is the burgeoning number of butterflies and hummingbirds that will soon be attracted to your garden. Most herb flowers are generous with their nectar, the sweet liquid bribe that flowers employ to lure their pollinators. As butterflies, hummingbirds, wasps, bees, and other insects visit flowers in search of nectar, they become dusted with pollen, which they then unwittingly transfer elsewhere to complete the fertilization of a flower. Mission accomplished, in the perspective of both participants.

IRRESISTIBLE BLOOMS

Red-flowered beebalm has such high hummingbird appeal that you can almost guarantee the presence of these zippy little birds by planting it, even if hummers have never before visited your garden. They also are quick to home in on culinary sage and other salvias, whose tubular nectar-filled blossoms are tailor-made for their long bills. Agastache is another hummingbird favorite.

Butterflies appreciate the clusters and spikes of small blossoms brimming with nectar on mints, goldenrod, and lots of other herbs.

Lavender flowers are highly favored by tiny, dainty blue butterflies. The clustered heads of oregano flowers attract butterflies big and small, which will jockey for feeding space in your herb bed. Large swallowtails and monarchs are drawn to the blossoms of purple coneflower, which provide a secure perch for the butterfly while it sips nectar from the many small petal-less flowers that make up the "eye" of the daisy. Late-blooming goldenrod is a mainstay on the menu of fall-migrating monarch butterflies.

Adult butterflies are also drawn to herbs that serve as the food of their finicky caterpillars, which eat only one or a very few kinds of plants. Black swallowtails, for example, will lay their pearly eggs on parsley, dill, and carrot foliage, where you can then observe the boldly striped caterpillars before they mature into the next generation of dancing wings. Vivid gold-and-brown fritillary butterflies seek violets to host their new brood. And if the leaves of your nasturtiums are looking nibbled, your garden may soon enjoy a fresh batch of lively cabbage white butterflies.

The more herb flowers your garden offers, the more nectar-seeking visitors you'll attract. But don't worry if your gardening space is limited: even a collection of potted herbs will attract hummingbirds and butterflies.

10 best herbs for hummingbirds and butterflies

agastache beebalm blazing star coneflower goldenrod hibiscus hyssop lavender rosemary salvias

5

herb directory

Meet dozens of old, new, and unusual herbs in this gallery section, which will introduce you to the personalities, needs, and uses of each plant. Throughout the chapter, the planting and cultivation information will address the issue of how to sow or plant each herb. If you are growing from seed, you can assume it is safe to sow directly into the ground outside unless the cultural advice suggests you start in pots. Similarly, pots can be placed either indoors or out, unless specified otherwise.

Achillea millefolium
yarrow

A favorite in perennial gardens, the 2- to 3-foot-tall yarrow has an airy feel, due to its feathery foliage, which gave it the old name of milfoil, or "thousand leaves." The white-flowered species, which escaped from gardens to grow wild, is a pretty plant for borders and cottage gardens. More refined, cultivated varieties bloom in soft salmon, pink, coppery red, and pale or butter yellow. All colors give a gentle multi-hued effect, as older blossoms soften to paler shades. One of the longest-blooming perennials, yarrow lends delicacy to larger-flowered companions like coneflower, shasta daisy, irises, and roses.

Yarrow flowers add lasting color to dried wreaths, bouquets, and potpourri, and the pungent leaves counteract oily skin or hair, and aid the healing of skin abrasions. Simmer 2 tbsp dried leaves in 1 cup water and use occasionally to rinse hair, splash an oily face, or apply to minor cuts and scrapes. Avoid repeated use, which may cause skin sensitivity or irritation.

planting Grow from seed or buy young plants. Adapts to most soil types; thrives in dry to slightly wet sites. Blooms most in full sun, but also part shade.

cultivation Snip off flowers before they set seed so it reblooms until late fall. Expands by spreading roots; propagate by division. May self-sow. Zones 2–8.

harvest Clip flower stems soon after blossoms open; hang to dry. Collect leaves anytime for drying on screens; store away from direct light.

Aconitum spp.
monkshood

Beautiful but deadly even in small doses, this is an herb for remembrance of times past, when the cure could be worse than the disease. Once a poison for wolves and rodents, the plant known as "wolfsbane" and "mousebane" may also have been more nefariously employed, as its literally heart-stopping toxin, aconite, works just as dramatically on two-legged animals.

For true-blue color and vertical height in the garden, this long-lived perennial is a trouble-free (although later blooming) alternative to finicky delphiniums. With stout stems of sharply lobed leaves topped by spires of deep blue, hooded flowers, monkshood may reach 6 feet tall, but needs no staking. The emphatic upright form and rich color are a dramatic contrast to asters, eupatoriums, 'Autumn Joy' sedum, and other late-season flowers of more relaxed personality. Grow monkshood in ornamental gardens, away from herbs and edibles, so there is no chance of misidentification and accidental usage.

planting Begin with grown plants; seed is very slow to start. Plant in fall, in average to fertile soil, full or part sun. Settle top of root just below the surface.
cultivation Consider as a lasting garden member; it is long-lived and hard to transplant. Divide the brittle roots every 3 to 4 years. Mulch to keep moist and cool. Grows best if nights remain cool. Zones 3–7.
harvest Poisonous. Wear gloves and avoid skin contact with all parts of the plant, especially the roots.

Acorus calamus
sweet flag

Resembling a stand of cattails rather than iris, sweet flag flourishes in swamps, streams, lakes, and other wet wild places across the Eastern half of North America. Its flat, grassy leaf blades shelter unusual green flower structures that jut out sideways, curving slightly upward. The phallic shape of the flower may be why old-time herbalists assigned it with aphrodisiac properties, celebrated in Walt Whitman's erotic "Calamus" poems. Before you're tempted to experiment, be aware that research shows that oil distilled from the roots may have carcinogenic properties when ingested.

Remarkably, this wetland-loving perennial also thrives in moist garden soil, although it looks most at home planted beside or in a garden pool or pond to add linear grace. Crush a leaf to sniff the spicy-sweet scent; the tuberous roots are also highly aromatic.

planting Start with grown plants. Plant in moist to wet soil, or water, in full to part sun. In smaller water gardens, keep sweet flag in the pot to stop it taking over too much territory via spreading roots.
cultivation Mulch deeply to keep soil cool and moist, if not planted directly in water or boggy soil. In large ponds, muskrats may dine on roots and shoots. Zones 3–9. 'Variegatus' is hardy in Zones 4–9.
harvest Dig roots in fall. Dry in a low-heat oven or outdoors on screens. Grind dried roots in blender or food processor. Do not use internally.

a soothing potion for the bath

Sweet flag is reputed to banish insomnia and help calm nervous tension. Try this relaxing addition to your before-bed bath; the delicious fragrance alone will help you forget the stress of the day.

3 tbsp dried roots, finely ground
1 quart water

Bring water to boil over a high heat. Stir in ground roots. Boil for about 1 minute, then remove from the heat and steep for 5 minutes. Strain out bits of root. Add the water to a tub of hot bath water, stirring to combine, and then settle in for a relaxing soak.

Agastache spp.
anise hyssop

A delight in all seasons, this perennial is suffused with a licorice scent. From summer through fall, anise hyssop is covered with fuzzy spikes of flowers that attract butterflies, hummingbirds, bumblebees, and other nectar-gatherers. Its soft blue-purple can partner most colors: try it with high-voltage red zinnias, lemon daylilies, or in a cool group of whites and blues. In winter, the dark, branching stems and seedheads stand out like candelabra. For an eyecatching off-season composition, combine with fountain grass (*Pennisetum* spp.), whose waterfall of bleached fall foliage makes a great winter backdrop for the bare, upright agastache.

Dried hyssop holds its color, so is ideal in arrangements or potpourri. Leaves make a fresh flavoring in tea, salad, and rice dishes. For more adventures, try giant hyssop or Korean mint (*A. rugosa*), Mexican giant hyssop (*A. mexicana*), and hybrid 'Tutti Frutti,' all good for tea.

planting Very easy to grow. Start from seed, buy young plants, or beg a cutting; roots easily in moist soil. Plant in full sun, in lean to fertile well-drained soil.

cultivation Short-lived. Divide in spring, or start cuttings in summer. Self-sows if seedheads are not removed; transplant seedlings or cover with mulch. Zones 6–10; other species or hybrids, Zones 8–10.

harvest Snip leaves anytime, to use fresh or air-dry. Cut flowers when they open and hang-dry, or chop as garnish. In winter, use stems for tea or potpourri.

Agrimonia eupatoria
agrimony

Agrimony escaped from colonial herb gardens long ago, and now thrives in woods, fields, and along roadsides across much of North America. If you enjoy walking on the wild side, you may have already made the acquaintance of this plant, whose barbed "sticktight" seeds are notorious for hitching a ride on passersby. But don't let this ingenious method of seed dispersal keep you from enjoying agrimony.

In summer, shade-loving agrimony holds delicate wands of yellow above its foliage, bringing color to green shade gardens, where it combines beautifully with ferns. This perennial herb was held in high esteem as nature's version of Tums. Not only did it quiet an acid stomach, it also relieved constipation and soothed aches and pains. Use it to refresh tired tootsies; steep 3 tsp of dried leaves in a cup of water and add to a footbath. Leaves and stems yield a rich yellow dye for yarn or cloth.

planting Easy to start from seed or young plants. Plant in partial to full shade, in any well-drained soil.

cultivation Keep this 4-footer away from paths, so its seeds don't grab unsuspecting visitors. Or snip off ripening seedheads and dispose of them to prevent hitchhiking or self-sowing. Zones 6–10.

harvest Collect leaves anytime for drying. For dye, snip off plant at base in late fall, cut into pieces, and simmer several handfuls in a stewpot for about an hour; strain out herbs and add yarn or fabric.

Alchemilla mollis
lady's mantle

Surprised to find a popular ornamental parading through a gallery of herbs? Nearly every plant under the sun has been tried for helpful uses, and lovely lady's mantle had its place in the natural pharmacy at one time. Supposedly, it encouraged blood to clot more quickly, making it useful for primitive tooth extractions, during menstrual difficulties, or after an unfortunate accident, whether wild animal attacks, border wars, or mishaps with the woodcutting ax.

Nowadays, it's safer and faster to call 911, but it's still nice to know that the pretty lady with the velvety leaves and billows of delicate flowers could come to the rescue in times of true desperation. If you want to experiment, mix young leaves in salads for a bitter tang, or infuse 2 tsp fresh leaves in 1 cup water to sip during that week of celebrating womanhood.

Make this versatile plant at home in perennial beds and borders, where she will mingle happily with bearded or Siberian iris, Oriental poppies, or any other flower needing a soft feminine touch. Try lady's mantle as an underplanting for your favorite rose, or let it spill over the edges of a path or wall. Some lady's mantle self-sows, but in America this perennial rarely sports seedlings. Be sure to admire it after rain, when its pleated foliage holds a net of fine droplets.

planting Seeds are hard to start. Buy young plants, and settle in moist but well-drained, fertile soil, full sun.
cultivation Propagate by division in spring; mild-winter areas can wait till fall. Clip the flowers when they fade for a fresh crop. Zones 3–7.
harvest Snip young leaves anytime to use fresh or dry.

Allium sativum
garlic

Garlic's ability to repel vampires is still open to investigation, but its medicinal successes make an astounding list. Tests have shown it reduces high blood pressure, thus making it a possible aid in preventing strokes. It is also effective at lowering blood sugar levels, an important step toward controlling diabetes. It may help to cure fungal infections, even those that crop up on fingernails and toenails and are difficult to remedy with modern medicines. Because garlic is reputed to boost the immune system, eating a clove or two a day may help ward off the common cold or flu. With all these benefits, a daily dose of garlic is nothing to sneeze at. So boil the pasta and peel those cloves!

Not only will garlic improve your health, it also livens up your cooking. Its robust oniony flavor has spread from Italian spaghetti

planting Plant in spring or early fall, in well-drained soil, full sun. Set individual cloves of garlic, pointed end up, about 4 inches apart and 2 inches deep.

cultivation Apply compost around plants and water regularly for bigger bulbs. All zones.

harvest When the tops bend over, usually by late summer, dig up the bulbs and "cure" on a screen or tabletop for about a week until excess water evaporates and the skin dries to paper. Wipe off soil, cut off roots with scissors, and store.

preserving garlic

Each clove you plant will yield a full, plump bulb of garlic at season's end, a bounty that may take you by surprise. Store them loosely in a cardboard box in a dark, dry place, or make a picturesque and time-honored garlic braid that will keep the herb within easy reach.

1 Consider the bulbs as the top of each strand, and the leaves as their bottoms.

2 Lay 3 bulbs side by side, and braid their leaves as 3 strands, crossing the left over the center, then right over center, then left over center. Repeat the pattern

to gourmet pizzas, roast chicken, and even all-American mashed potatoes—in fact, just about everything but dessert. The intense flavor turns mild with longer cooking, which is why "Fifty-Clove Chicken" is not a frightening recipe but a mouth-watering one. Whole bulbs are a nutty-sweet treat when roasted; each clove yields a soft pulp that you can squeeze into your mouth.

Snuggle the strappy, dark green leaves of garlic into ornamental gardens, where their pungent odor reputedly deters whiteflies and other pests. Allow easy access for harvesting both the bulbs and the leafy tops, which contribute flavor to eggs, stirfries, and other quick dishes. The white or pinkish flowers are also edible. Tone down garlic breath by eating fresh parsley or mint; remove garlic odor from fingers by rubbing mint between them.

Allium schoenoprasum
chives

How bored our tastebuds would be without the fabulous family of onions! Big brother 'Vidalia' and robust garlic may garner most of the glory, but chives are just as valuable at waking up the flavors of foods, and their finer leaves and showier flowers are much prettier in the ornamental garden. Use them to outline a path, to mark corners, or to dot a flower bed with vertical accents. Their pink-purple blossoms appear in late spring and last into early summer, making chives a good companion for the wave of irises and roses that grace the garden at its peak. There's a sneaky practical reason for inviting chives into your perennial border, too: like garlic, the aromatic leaves are believed to repel insect pests. If you're fighting Japanese beetles, it can't hurt to enlist a crop of these soldiers on your side.

until the braided section is about 2 inches long—the size of a garlic bulb.

3 Lay another 3 bulbs on top of the braided section. Combine the new bulbs' leaves with those of the old bulbs, so that you still have three separate strands.

4 Braid as before until the section is, once more, about 2 inches long. Repeat Steps 2 and 3 until the desired length.

5 Knot the loose ends, trim the excess, and hang with the original 3 bulbs at the base. Cut from bottom as required.

planting Start chives from seed in pots, sowing thickly on the surface of moist potting mix; the seedlings look like ultra-thin blades of new grass. Or start with young potted plants. Plant in full sun, in average to fertile, well-drained soil. Also good in pots, and on indoor windowsills.

cultivation Water regularly. Cut back hard in midsummer for fresh, new growth. Self-sows, but extras are always welcome. Zones 3–9.

harvest Snip tops regularly, cutting off just above soil level. Use fresh for best flavor. Cut edible flowers soon after opening. Sniff the blooms—their scent is surprisingly sweet, although their taste is oniony.

Allium spp.
alliums

If you grew up in the Appalachian mountains, you may have tried ramps, the powerful wild onion of eastern American woods. Or perhaps you've detected a garlicky smell after mowing the lawn, as clumps of European wild garlic get cut with the grass. Maybe you've seen "pregnant onion" as a houseplant, with tiny bulbs produced atop its stems. Dedicated flower gardeners may also have played with *Allium moly*, a delicate charmer with liberal butter-yellow blooms, or the huge purple lollipops of *A. giganteum*. The genus includes onions, shallots, leeks, garlic, and chives, as well as hundreds of lesser known treasures. It's likely many alliums share the beneficial properties of some members, but until the jury is in, explore as ornamental herbs.

planting Grow from purchased bulbs, as directed.
cultivation Varies according to species.
harvest Keep as flowers unless you are sure the variety is edible.

Aloe vera
aloe

Aloe has been getting good press for thousands of years—and its reputation as a healing herb still holds true today. Ancient armies used it to treat battle wounds, while modern medicine employs it to treat burns from cancer radiation treatments. Soothing and antiseptic, aloe gel heals minor burns, scrapes, cuts, and other skin blemishes. Skin mends faster, with less scarring, and pain or itching are instantly relieved. Try it on patches of sunburn, poison ivy rashes, and mosquito bites, or use it to help clear up acne, dandruff, and oily skin.

A tender plant, aloe melts to mush at the nip of frosty temperatures. In cold regions, grow in pots and use as a patio plant. In hotter spots, enjoy it in the garden. Its bold cluster of fleshy, spiky leaves and flowers contrast well with sprawling sedums and hold their own by cacti.

No matter where you garden, keep a potted aloe in the kitchen, and another near the outdoor grill, where you can break off a leaf to wipe on any burns from cooking mishaps. The sooner you apply it, the less damage your skin will incur.

Fresh aloe gel is most potent. Simply snap off a piece of leaf about 2 inches long and split with your fingernail to expose the thick, juicy sap. Dab or smear the gel straight on the skin and let it dry, or use gauze to hold the leaf in place.

Originally hailing from desert regions of Africa, aloe takes in its stride heat, dry air, and even lack of water, indoors or out. You can leave for vacation with a free conscience, because aloe can go weeks without water, pulling the liquid it needs from its succulent leaves. Give it a generous drink to make its leaves quickly plump up again, ready for use.

planting Buy a young plant, or ask a friend for a start. Plant in full sun to light shade, in well-drained soil, or grow in containers.

cultivation Aloe grows fast and needs little care. The plant multiplies quickly, producing "babies," or offshoots, around the base of the parent. Potted plants flourish even when the roots are crowded. To propagate, pinch off the offshoots and plant each baby aloe in a new pot. Zone 10.

harvest Break off pieces as needed; the broken end will quickly heal over. To obtain larger quantities of gel, break off large leaves at their base, collecting no more than half the leaves from a single plant.

make your own healing potion

1 Thoroughly wash, rinse, and dry a small, wide-mouthed jar with a snap-on or screw-on lid. The squat glass jars from specialty mustards, for example, are ideal.

2 Break off about 6 to 10 large leaves from your aloe plant, pinching or else slicing them off at the base.

3 Working on a non-absorbent cutting board, slit a leaf down the center with a sharp paring knife. Hold the leaf over a small bowl and press the gelatinous juice out of the leaf and into the bowl, using the back of your thumbnail.

4 Slit and extract the juice from the other leaves, working on one at a time. Scrape the collected juice into the jar, using a small flexible bowl scraper. Label the jar and store in the refrigerator. Apply to skin or scalp as needed.

summer refreshers

On hot summer days, lemon scent is a quick pick-me-up. Try a full menu of lemon verbena: iced tea and cookies, followed by a citrusy soak or splash.

Steep beebalm and lemon verbena leaves, strain, and pour over ice. Accompany with butter cookies (storebought cookies are a sneaky time-saver), glazed with icing made from ½ cup confectioners' sugar, 2 tsp hot milk, and ¼ tsp vanilla. Sprinkle finely chopped lemon verbena atop each cookie before the glaze dries. Afterward, splash your face with leftover tea diluted with an equal amount of cold water, or pour 1 cup into a warm bath.

Aloysia triphylla
lemon verbena

The clean, lively scent of lemon is as irresistible in food and drink as it is in cosmetics and room fresheners, so use lemon verbena with abandon in teas, cooking, or any herbal craft. Spice up your garden by placing pots near a bench, beside a gate, or on the deck, where guests can enjoy the delicious scent of the foliage when they brush against it or reach out and rub a leaf.

This gracefully branched perennial herb is happy in containers and grows vigorously in the garden. Reaching 2 feet tall and wide, with stems that turn woody with age, it makes an excellent anchor for lemon-scented collections. Underplant the willowy-leaved verbena with a mat of diminutive lemon thyme or creeping mother-of-thyme for a pair of pleasing herbs that look and taste good together. Lemon verbena can't tolerate the touch of frost, but it will quickly grow to a good-sized plant in a single garden season, even in cold-winter areas.

planting Seed is difficult to germinate; start with a young plant. Grow in full sun, in well-drained soil.

cultivation Fertilize to boost leafy growth. Water regularly to prevent leaf drop. To overwinter indoors, cut back by about half and move to a sunny window. Propagate by cuttings. Zones 8–11.

harvest Gather leaves anytime for fresh use or drying. Snip leafy branch tip or entire branches. If you don't intend to overwinter the plant, cut at ground level before frost and dry for later use.

Anethum graveolens
dill

Pungent and distinctive in aroma and flavor, this feathery annual herb is as easy to grow as marigolds. Even a single plant produces a bounty of leaves and seeds to add piquancy to main dishes and side salads, and of course to pickles, probably the number one use of dill. Its clusters of tiny flowers attract beneficial pest-controlling insects to your garden to protect other plants, and its ferny greens are munched by the boldly striped caterpillars of the black swallowtail butterfly.

Tall in height but with a delicate personality, dill plants bring a filmy softness to their garden companions. Try a patch of dill with red-hot zinnias or giant lemon-yellow marigolds, or let the self-sown progeny spring up to add airy grace among deep blue salvias and other perennials. For a thoroughly modern use of this time-honored herb, incorporate chartreuse dill flowers into a modern color scheme of burgundy-leaved dahlias and lime-green sweet potato vine, or you could use fresh or dried flowers in arrangements.

Dill sprouts and matures quickly, so for a longer display in the garden or a continual supply of fresh "dillweed," sow in successive plantings, about two weeks apart throughout the growing season. Even seedlings carry the trademark taste, so are good in a simple yogurt-dill dressing for cucumbers, or strewn across salmon and other fish.

planting Utterly foolproof from seeds sown directly in the garden. Grow in full sun, in well-drained soil.

cultivation Fertile soil or generous fertilizer produces a leafier, taller plant. Clip off seedheads before ripe to prevent self-sowing, or smother unwanted seedlings with mulch. Do not transplant. All zones.

harvest Cut leaves, flowers, and seedheads with scissors. Collect leaves and flowers anytime. Use fresh or dried, or freeze leafy stems in zip-top bags and snip, while frozen, into recipes. Shake seeds into a bag, and rub seedheads to remove any left.

Angelica archangelica
angelica

Evil witches supposedly steer clear of angelica, whose very name evokes the forces of good. But if you've ever tried to start it from seed, you may have felt ready to side with the sinister instead of the angels. Its reputation as temperamental to start is deserved: the seeds lose viability after only a few months. Young plants can be tricky, too, because the taproot sulks if disturbed.

It's worth repeated tries to get this statuesque herb into the garden. Its stout, attractive leaves and chin-high stems have a powerful presence, and when the plant blooms, its big greenish-white flowerheads shine across the yard like spotlights. Besides, once you have it, it will crop up year after year as it sows its own successors.

The licorice-flavored roots have been used to flavor alcohol, but frequent or large internal doses may cause paralysis of the nervous system—a side effect you definitely want to avoid! The stems are safe to eat sparingly as "candied angelica," which is simmered in sugar.

planting Buy fresh seeds in late summer or fall, and scatter on prepared soil immediately. Do not cover seeds. Grows in the sun or shade.
cultivation A biennial, angelica forms a clump of big leaves its first year and flowers, sets seed, and dies its second year. Learn to recognize seedlings to avoid pulling out self-starters. Zones 4–9.
harvest Cut the honey-scented flowers anytime to make fresh arrangements.

Anthriscus cerefolium
chervil

The subtle flavor of chervil is easy to overlook in the rush to fill gardens with familiar favorites. Its understated, slightly weedy form—like an anemic Queen Anne's lace—doesn't help make it a standout, either. So why grow it? Ask any devotee of French cooking—chervil is a member of the culinary melange called "fines herbes," valued for adding delicate, fresh flavor to sauces, soups, eggs, and cheese dishes.

The flavor of chervil is a hard-to-describe blend of faint licorice and mild parsley. Some say chervil adds "warmth" to recipes, perhaps because of that comforting aroma of anise. As a stand-alone player, it transforms steamed fresh peas or ordinary scrambled eggs into culinary bliss. It also is indispensable in the making of any self-respecting béarnaise sauce.

An infusion of chervil may be used in the hope of lowering blood pressure, although this claim is not yet recognized medically. It is also alleged to help prevent wrinkles!

planting Simple from seed scattered on prepared soil. Plant in sun to part shade, in well-drained soil.
cultivation This annual plant matures quickly; sow every two weeks for a constant supply. Pinch or clip off flowers to get a longer harvest of leaves from the plant. Self-sows generously; use unwanted seedlings in cooking and salads. All zones.
harvest Collect leaves anytime. Use fresh; the delicate flavor quickly diminishes when leaves are dried.

Arctium lappa
burdock

Proving that every plant has a silver lining, burdock leaps from the vacant lot to the herb garden, where you can appreciate the ornamental aspect of its rugged, ruffled leaves as well as the curative power of its root—and then dig it out before it gets a chance to set those prickly round burrs that cling so easily to your pets and clothes.

Burdock is one of the many foreign "weeds" that have made themselves at home in America, either by invitation or by accident. In the case of this herb, it's probably a little of both. Tea made from burdock roots was a popular cure for stomach ailments, so colonists may have brought the plant with them for use in their new homeland. The barbed seed coverings also no doubt came aboard, tangled in the wool of sheep or other livestock bound for the New World, accomplishing their task of seed dispersal admirably well once they reached hospitable soil.

planting Grows easily from seed. Look for burdock near walls where it escaped the lawnmower, or in unused parts of the garden. Thrives in sun or shade.

cultivation A biennial, it remains a ground-hugging cluster of leaves its first year. The next summer, a stem of purple flowers emerges, the seeds mature into brown burrs, and the plant dies. Zones 3–9.

harvest Pick leaves as needed. Dig roots in fall of the second year, before seeds mature.

quick fix for an itch

Fresh burdock leaves may help soothe the itch of poison ivy, poison oak, or even a bad case of mosquito bites. Break off a fresh leaf and crumble it lightly in your hands to bruise the surface and leaf veins. Straighten out the leaf and lay it directly on the irritated skin. Hold the burdock leaf in place for a few minutes, then discard.

Armoracia rusticana
horseradish

One good sniff is enough to test horseradish root's abilities to instantly clear stuffy sinuses. This powerful plant is a member of the mustard family, a large group of plants that share a similar peppery tang. Spurned by animals of the equine persuasion, horseradish gets its name from its coarse, or "horsey," characteristics. Its thick leaves can grow up to 2 feet long; they form a clump that may measure 3 feet across in less than two seasons of growth and which never stops expanding. Underground, the knobby brown roots may stretch as deep as 2 feet.

As a condiment, horseradish root is unparalleled for adding zing to beef, corned beef, salmon, creamcheese spreads, potato salad, and meat loaf. Mix a bit into mayonnaise-based dressings to give mild-mannered tuna salad or avocados an unexpected spicy bite, or to spread on sandwiches of deli meats or cheeses. Scallops, shrimp, and faux or real crabmeat also make a good vehicle for horseradish, either in a white sauce or mixed with catsup for popular cocktail sauce.

Away from the table, horseradish comes in handy for cold, sinus, or allergy problems that make breathing difficult; just inhale a whiff to clear your head. Its stimulant effect may give some relief to achy or arthritic joints or overtired muscles; spread freshly grated root on a cotton handkerchief and lay on the stiff or sore area.

planting Treat as permanent and give it a corner you won't mind it taking over; it is tough to get rid of once established, as each little piece of root left in the soil will sprout anew. Plant purchased root in sun to part shade, in well-drained soil.

cultivation Mulch to control weeds and keep the soil moist for digging. Zones 2–10.

harvest Dig roots in late summer to early fall. Store roots in the refrigerator to maintain fresh flavor.

two quick & easy horseradish sauces

for sandwiches

1 Peel a 3- to 4-inch piece of fresh root with a sharp paring knife. Grate it manually on a medium to fine grater or else use a food processor.

2 Empty a small jar of commercial mayonnaise into a mixing bowl. Stir in the horseradish one tablespoon at a time, until the spiciness is to your liking. Spoon into a jar and store in the refrigerator. It will keep for months.

for smoked or pickled fish

1 Peel a 1- to 2-inch piece of fresh root with a sharp paring knife. Grate on a medium to fine grater or use a food processor.

2 Combine horseradish, 1 cup low-fat sour cream, ½ tsp Dijon-style mustard, and a pinch of salt. Let the flavors meld for half an hour before serving. Spread on steamed or baked fish, or serve as a side sauce. Also delicious with hot or cold roast beef.

Artemisia spp.
artemisias

Silvery leaves are the hallmark of this genus, a group of aromatic plants that includes wormwood (*A. absinthium*, see upper right), once used in the making of a liqueur whose delirium-inducing effects were immortalized in Degas' painting *The Absinthe Drinkers*. If absinthe isn't your cup of tea, how about vermouth? Wormwood also gave that drink its signature flavor, before the herb's use was outlawed because of its toxic effects.

Strongly bitter in smell and taste, wormwood once enjoyed wide use as a treatment for intestinal worms, a flea repellent, and a deterrent to mice and book lice. In a desperate attempt to ward off the Plague, some folks rubbed their bodies with wormwood; although artemisias do have germ-killing properties, wormwood unfortunately can cause severe dermatitis in susceptible individuals.

On the brighter side, artemisias are pretty plants, with billows of pale foliage that can be as fine as lace. Use as hedges, clipped or natural, and as backdrops for white or colored flowers. The ghostly foliage, held year round in most species, is an effective highlight with red-leaved barberry and other plants of burgundy hue, and with the mellow golds of wintertime ornamental grasses. The sprays of tiny gray or yellowish flowers (see bottom right) tend to be overshadowed by the foliage.

planting Start with young plants or cuttings, which root quickly in moist soil. Plant in full to part sun or light shade, in well-drained soil.

cultivation Drought tolerant; great in containers or the garden (but beware spreading roots). Cut back by half in late winter to foster new growth. Zones 3–10.

harvest Don't use medicinally. Pick leaves or branches anytime for drying. Use as an insect repellent in closets and pet bedding, or in dried arrangements. If you like the scent, use sparingly in potpourri.

Artemisia tridentata
sacred sage, sagebrush

Sagebrush grows so thickly on western plains and deserts that it makes the landscape look gray. Up close, you may see pronghorn antelope stepping among the woody-stemmed plants, or jackrabbits lolling in their shade. The silvery leaves of *A. tridentata* (also called *Seriphidium tridentatum*) and other artemisias are adapted to save water; less moisture is lost to evaporation.

This perennial herb has been widely used and well treasured for centuries. Strongly aromatic as well as symbolic, sage was used by native Americans in religious ceremonies, cleansing rituals, blessings or banishings, and in more pragmatic matters, such as pest control and medical treatment. When a fire was needed, sagebrush flared quickly and burned brightly.

In recent years, "smudge sticks" made from sage have become a cottage industry in the herb's native habitat. The slow-burning, tightly packed sticks are used in ceremonies based on ancient traditions or modern spiritual variations.

planting Start with young plants or cuttings, which root easily in moist soil. Plant in full sun, in well-drained soil.

cultivation Sage does best in dry climates, but feel free to experiment with it no matter where you live, to bring a bit of the Old West home. Zones 3–9.

harvest Clip branches or leaves for drying anytime, even winter. Use in fresh or dried arrangements, or in potpourri. If the almost camphor-like fragrance is pleasing to your nose, slip a sprig of sage between stored wool blankets or sweaters to repel moths.

Artemisia dracunculus 'Sativa'
French tarragon

Ordinary chicken salad becomes a specialty of the house when you mix chopped tarragon into the mayonnaise, and fish is sublime with a tarragon-infused sauce. Use it to dress up canned soups, or scatter chopped leaves on rice or roasted potatoes. Tarragon turns bitter if it's cooked in dry heat, so use it in sauces or other liquids, or add it near the end of cooking.

If you find yourself nodding off afterward, you may be experiencing its reputed ability to beat insomnia. Try tarragon tea for a sleepytime treat.

planting Buy a young plant. Tarragon seedlings vary greatly in their aromatic value. Plant in full sun, in light, well-drained soil.

cultivation Do not fertilize; a lean diet makes the flavors more intense. Water container-grown plants regularly, but make sure the potting mix drains quickly; soggy soil will cause a quick decline. Propagate by division in early spring. Zones 4–8.

harvest Clip leaves and sprigs anytime, for fresh use or freezing. Use for flavored oils and vinegars, and in fresh and dried arrangements.

beware of impostors

The strong taste of French tarragon (*A. dracunculus* 'Sativa') is complex—sweet, lively, and redolent of licorice. The lookalike, *A. dracunculus*, often labeled Russian tarragon, is insipid, with little scent or flavor. Before you buy, rub and sniff a leaf.

Bellis perennis
English daisy

Dainty white or rosy pink English daisies bloom in early spring with the first dandelions. In mild areas, the charming little flowers may dot the lawn all winter. They're a foreign invader from Europe and now escaped from flower gardens into backyards in the Pacific Northwest, the Northeast, and other cooler areas of the country.

That dainty daisy packs a lot of power in its inch-wide blossoms. Made into a tea or infusion, the flowers have been used for generations to heal inflammations and burns, to relieve colds and coughs, and as a gentle laxative.

In the garden, English daisies are the perfect companion for early spring bulbs. Try a light or deep pink variety with pale pink hyacinths and silver-and-burgundy ajuga. Let them self-sow between paving stones in walks and patios, or anywhere else they decide to spring up. They are happy campers in container gardens, too, where you can feature their cheerful flowers in a wide, shallow bowl, or crowd them around the rim of a big clay pot of blue pansies and white daffodils.

planting Start from seed or buy young plants already in bud. Plant in sun to part shade in moist soil.
cultivation English daisies have an exceptionally long bloom period, often lasting for several months. For more daisies in the lawn, let the flowers mature into seed before mowing the lawn. Zones 3–10.
harvest Pluck flowers soon after the buds open, and dry for use in teas and infusions.

casual daisies by design

A sprinkling of daisies in the spring grass looks so natural, it couldn't possibly have been planned—could it? Sure! Start a patch of English daisies from a packet of seed in a nursery bed in spring. In fall, transplant the young perennials into your lawn after the final mowing. Your new daisies will bloom the following spring and for years thereafter.

Borago officinalis
borage

An all-purpose wonder drug in the herbalist's kit, borage is also beloved by beekeepers, cooks, and gardeners for its ample, true-blue blossoms.

Medicinal research indicates borage has promise for treating diverse ailments, including arthritis, acne, eczema, fever, premenstrual syndrome, and possibly multiple sclerosis. It may also help hangovers and weight loss. Its healing powers are attributed to gamma-linolenic acid, also found in evening primrose. Its leaves add cool, fruity flavor to salads, spreads, and dips. The flowers are edible and healthy, too, so sprinkle them atop salads or float in a cold fruit soup. To heal skin break-outs, pour boiling water over 2 cups fresh leaves, make a towel tent over your head, and steam your face for ten minutes.

The large, simple leaves of borage contrast well with plants of finer-textured foliage. Simple from seed, this 2-foot-tall annual makes a pretty partner for chives, shasta daisies, lady's mantle (*Alchemilla mollis*), and pink evening primrose.

flowers in ice

Everyday ice water goes elegant when you add bright blue starry flowers to the beverage. Instead of floating them in the drinks, where they will interfere with sipping, freeze them in ice cubes. Just drop a pretty borage blossom into each section of your ice cube tray, fill with water and freeze, and then serve as usual.

planting Sprinkle seed on bare soil in a sunny site in lean to fertile, well-drained soil.

cultivation Self-sows generously. Smother unwanted seedlings with mulch, or plant in a cottage garden. The flowers are beloved by honeybees; keep it away from paths to avoid stings. Annual; all zones.

harvest Gather leaves and blossoms anytime for fresh use. Chop or slice young leaves for culinary use; steam older leaves for tea or facials.

Calendula officinalis
pot marigold, calendula

Contemplating calendulas was a sure cure for the doldrums, said herbalists in medieval times, and who could disagree? The intense golden orange hue of this old favorite is as welcome as sunshine. Within those pretty petals lie healing powers, too, because calendula blossoms are antibacterial, antifungal, and antiseptic—three properties that make them useful for healing wounds, treating pimples and other infections, and making pesky warts disappear.

Calendula petals look just as cheerful in foods as they do in the garden, so use them for a dash of color in green salads, potato or pasta salads, and soups. Or sprinkle the petals on cake icings, for a delightful springtime dessert.

A lover of cool weather, calendula blooms best in spring and fall where summers are hot. It will keep blooming even after moderately heavy frosts, and in mild regions, it may last all winter. Like the popular daylily 'Stella d'Oro,' it has a brassy tint that can be tricky to combine with flowers of other colors. Cultivated varieties of gentler hues are available, but the sunny orange of the species jazzes up the garden and looks great with gray-foliaged herbs. In flowerbeds, choose partners of deep purple, true blue, white, yellow, or rusty red. Unless you particularly like clashing colors, avoid planting calendula next to magenta flowers like 'Purple Wave' petunia; use white-flowered or silvery plants between such strong personalities for a less jolting effect.

planting Sow seed in fall for earliest spring flowering, or buy a multipack of plants in bud and bloom. Plant in full sun to part shade, in well-drained soil of lean to rich fertility.

cultivation Expect pot marigolds to look tired and bedraggled during the long, hot summer, then perk up when the days shorten and the nights cool. Mildew may whiten leaves but isn't fatal; cut off affected parts. Good in mild-winter or spring windowboxes. Drought tolerant. Self-sows moderately. Annual; all zones.

harvest Pick fresh flowers anytime. Pluck off the petals for use in food.

Capsella bursa-pastoris
shepherd's purse

Many of the weeds growing unnoticed by the wayside are escapees from old-time gardens, brought to America by Old World settlers. The common weed called shepherd's purse is most noticeable when its tiny white flowers have transformed into the spikes of seedpods that give the plant its name. Look closely and you'll see each little pod looks like a three-cornered or heart-shaped pouch, a miniature version of the leather bag holding cheese, bread, and perhaps a sip of wine shepherds would take to the fields.

Shepherd's purse has long been gathered for spring greens, eaten boiled, blanched, or raw as a pick-me-up in springtime. After a long winter without fresh greens, this unassuming plant offered a welcome dose of vitamins A and C. Its flavor is mildly peppery, with a hint of cabbage. Herbalists also used the plant to staunch bleeding, encourage labor contractions during childbirth, and ease menstrual difficulties.

planting Shepherd's purse may already be growing in your yard or gardens. If not, collect seedpods along roadsides and sprinkle on bare soil in full sun.
cultivation Restrict to herb garden to avoid weed problem. Pull self-sown seedlings with a twisting motion, to loosen deep taproot. Annual; all zones.
harvest Pick fresh leaves in late winter to early spring. Because it may constrict blood vessels, sample only in small quantities, and avoid ingesting this herb if you take blood-thinning medication.

Capsicum frutescens
cayenne pepper

Christopher Columbus first met cayenne pepper as a shrub in his explorations of tropical America, where it often grows to a height of 3 feet or more, with a stout, woody trunk. In cold winter gardens, we know cayenne as a bushy foot-high plant that bears abundant red peppers, then tends to die when the cold weather sets in. Rating relatively low on the spiciness scale, unlike the five-alarm habanero, cayenne is perfect for spicing up your chili or burgers, pasta, eggs, and curries.

It is capsaicin that gives hot peppers their heat. Extracted commercially, this substance is used in creams to relieve the pain of shingles and arthritis. Don't try to produce these treatments at home, though, as homemade salves can blister the skin.

Try capsaicin as a pest repellent for garden insects and those greedy squirrels at the bird feeder: soak a few handfuls of chopped peppers in a bucket of water for 24 hours and spray on plants or birdseed.

Herbalists used cayenne pepper to stimulate the appetite: whether that effect was due to its inherent compounds or to the way it livens up the flavor of food is a question you can research at your own table. More tacos, anyone?

pick a peck of peppers (pain-free harvesting)

Hot peppers are so powerful they can blister the skin—and you don't even want to think about what happens when capsaicin gets into the eyes. That's why it's essential to handle with care when picking and preparing hot peppers. Cover your hands with rubber gloves, wear a long-sleeved shirt, and above all, resist the urge to scratch an itch on unprotected skin, nose, or eyes.

Also take care when removing the gloves: slip your first ungloved hand into a plastic sandwich bag to pull off the second. The sandwich bag trick is fast and easy when adding hot peppers to food, too; use it to protect your hand when you pull a pepper from the braid or crumble a dried pod into the pot.

planting Sow seed indoors in late winter or buy young plants in late spring. After danger of frost plant in full sun, in well-drained average to fertile soil.

cultivation Good in containers; combine with dwarf red or yellow zinnias or dahlias. May be wintered indoors in bright light. Grow as annual, all zones; perennial, Zones 10–11.

harvest Snip off ripe red pods, leaving about half an inch of stem attached. Spread on screens to dry, or string through the stems, using a sturdy needle and carpet thread. Grind to powder in a food processor (wear a mask to avoid inhaling dust).

Carthamus tinctorius
safflower

Travel through the farmland of the Upper Midwest in summer, and you'll see thousands of acres of safflower glowing deep yellow–orange, like a giant pool of melted butter. Those massive plantings hold the makings for safflower oil, used by cooks since the days of the Pharaohs. Safflower is also prized for attracting bright red cardinals, and birdseed is big business today.

Accent corners of green herb gardens with bright safflower, or use it to complement blue salvias or Russian sage (*Perovskia atriplicifolia*). Safflower blossoms keep their color when dried, so they're perfect for everlasting arrangements. Use the petals to add color to salads and other dishes, or simmer them in sauces, soups, and curries to add a reddish orange tint. The blossoms yield dyes of rich yellow, rusty red, and brassy gold, depending on the substance used as a mordant to fix the color.

safflower silk scarf

1 Buy a lightweight white silk scarf, or finish a length of white silk with a narrow hem.

2 Combine 2–3 gallons water and ½–1 gallon safflower blossoms in a big cookpot. Bring to the boil, then simmer for about half an hour until the water is intensely colored. Cool and strain out the flowers.

3 Meanwhile, handwash the silk in Woolite. Rinse thoroughly.

4 Add the scarf to the dye bath and simmer for an hour. Rinse in very warm water, then cooler water, and finally cold water until the rinse runs clear. Hang in the shade to dry, then iron and wear proudly.

planting Sow seed in spring; soak overnight in a saucer of water to speed germination. Plant in a sunny site in lean to fertile soil.

cultivation Tolerates drought. A colorful touch for large containers; try with bright purslane or rose moss (*Portulaca* spp.) for a low-care patio pot. For continued bloom, clip flowers. Annual; all zones.

harvest Cut flowers soon after they open. Hang to dry, or put in arrangements and allow to dry in place. Inexpensive floral picks, from hobby or discount stores, can support the flowerheads in bouquets.

Carum carvi
caraway

Caraway and rye bread have been companions for centuries, but the nutty, licorice tang of this annual or biennial herb also infuses aquavit and kummel liqueurs, as well as sauerkraut, split pea soup, and Hungarian goulash. For a quick and savory side dish, sprinkle halved baked potatoes with Swiss cheese and caraway seeds during the last 15 minutes of baking. In Indian cuisine, the seeds are stirred into dishes and also offered after the meal, both for their palate-cleansing effect and their soothing, flatulence-eliminating properties. The brown seeds are most often used, but the taproot is edible, too.

Sow airy, delicate caraway in patches in the herb garden so it doesn't get lost in the crowd of more stalwart plants. Once planted, you'll always have a supply, because some seeds are always overlooked in harvest. These will then plant themselves in various nooks of the garden.

planting Sow seeds in average to fertile soil, in full sun. If you have caraway seed in your kitchen spice rack, simply sprinkle some in the garden.

cultivation Water during dry spells for best flowering and thus more seeds. Pull unwanted seedlings with a twisting motion to free taproot, and slice roots in salads or soups. Annual or biennial; all zones.

harvest Monitor plants to collect seeds after they ripen to brown but before they fall. Shake into a paper bag, or cut and hang upside down over a cardboard tray; they'll fall out when fully ripe.

Cassia / *Senna marilandica*
senna

Lewis and Clark carried senna in their medicine bag on their trek across America for the same reason you can find it in many over-the-counter remedies today: the plant is a powerful laxative. It's also a striking member of the herb garden, where its unusual foliage and intriguing yellow flowers rise on stems that may reach 6 feet tall. In winter, the flat, brown seedpods catch the eye and the ear, as they shift and rattle in the wind.

Plant senna to add shrub-like stature to your garden without creating the dense shade of a shrub. This long-lived perennial is also interesting enough to stand alone as a specimen at the center of intersecting paths. Underplant with golden-leaved thyme or golden oregano, to play up senna's yellow flowers in summer.

Homegrown senna is too unpredictable and powerful to use internally, but a mild infusion (1 tsp leaves steeped in 1 cup boiling water for half an hour) may be used as a mouthwash to counteract halitosis and garlic breath.

planting Start with young plants. Plant in well-drained lean to fertile soil, in full sun to light shade. Grows equally well in light, stony soils and dense clay.

cultivation Drought tolerant. Cut back any dead stalks to ground level after leaves appear. Zones 4–10.

harvest Gather leaves when flowers are in bloom, midsummer to early fall. Use fresh or dried. For a wall decoration, press a leaf with its oval leaflets in a thick book, and mount in a simple frame when dry.

Catharanthus roseus
Madagascar periwinkle

For a sun-baked spot where nothing else will grow—along a white masonry wall or house foundation in full sun, for instance—the vivid, abundant flowers of Madagascar periwinkle are just the prescription. This reliable tender perennial soaks up sun and heat, goes without water, and never flags. It's understandably one of the most popular bedding plants in recent years.

Eye-popping colors that shine like a spotlight across the garden are another benefit of this adaptable performer. Many cultivars sport dark "eyes" at the center of each flower, with white or pastel petals. The foliage is a deep, rich green and the plants fill out into thick, lush growth that knits together into a solid cloak of flower-topped greenery. Bloom begins in early summer and keeps going to frost, or through mild winters.

Madagascar periwinkle may prove to be a powerful drug in modern medicines for all kinds of conditions, but this is not a plant to play

modern miracles

Madagascar periwinkle may well turn out to be a miracle drug. The plant contains no less than 60 alkaloids, substances that hold promise for treating many of our most serious health problems. Extracts are already being used to treat childhood leukemia, testicular cancer, and Hodgkin's disease, a cancer of the immune system. It may also hold promise for victims of AIDS and Parkinson's disease.

Because of its powerful approach to slowing growth of tumors, Madagascar periwinkle has similar side effects to other regimens of cancer chemotherapy. It first attracted modern medical attention for its use as a diabetes treatment in Jamaica. Although not in general use in America, the plant shows some effect at lowering blood sugar in diabetics. It also helps reduce blood pressure.

around with. Even in old herbal lore, it was well respected as a poison, although it was administered in small doses to soothe asthma, consumption, tuberculosis, and the common cold. Scientists today are investigating its potential in many varied treatments, from chemotherapy to reducing blood pressure.

Another risky use of Madagascar periwinkle was as an agent to induce euphoria. Unfortunately, the induced feeling of well-being was often followed by serious aftereffects, including death.

Found in hot regions around the globe, the plant adapts easily as an annual in cold-winter gardens. Use it to line pathways, to edge patios, and to fill difficult areas with bright color. It's perfect in windowboxes and patio containers.

planting Buy inexpensive multipacks or potted plants in spring. Can also be grown from seed started indoors in winter. Grow in sun, in well-drained soil of almost any kind.

cultivation No care needed. Blooms continually until stopped by frost. If plants get leggy, cut back by a third to induce branching and compact growth.

harvest Do not use medicinally; highly poisonous when taken internally. Clip stems for fresh bouquets. Snip individual flowers for pressing.

Centranthus ruber
red valerian, jupiter's beard

Too showy to stay in the herb garden, the branching sprays of this perennial herb have migrated to ornamental gardens, where they add a luxuriant splash of color along paths or in beds with iris, Asiatic lilies, and other summer bloomers. Butterfly gardeners also adore this easy-to-grow plant, because its red, pink, or white flowers attract crowds of nectar-seekers. Even when not in bloom, red valerian garners attention because its smooth, pale gray-green leaves look so inviting to touch.

The thick, hefty root was once used in herbal remedies for the catch-all categories of "nervous disorders" and "hysteria." Like true valerian, it has a sedative effect. But don't try this at home: an overdose can be fatal, and even recommended recipes can have unfortunate effects. Calm your nerves by sniffing the sweet fragrance of the flowers and meditating on the butterflies that dance about the blossoms.

planting Start from seed sown in pots, or buy young plants. Plant in full sun, in fast-draining soil. Grows well in lean or alkaline soil.

cultivation Red valerian thrives on adversity. It blooms like mad in gravel and finds every niche in a stone wall. Good for coastal gardens. Self-sows abundantly, often forsaking pampered gardens to spring up in the stony spots it likes best. Zones 5–9.

harvest Enjoy the fresh flowers in bouquets. Do not ingest the bitter leaves or root.

Chamaemelum nobile
chamomile

Whether you say "chamomile" or "camomeal" (both are correct), this herb's name is one of the most familiar to gardeners and nongardeners alike. Good for upsets both physical and mental, chamomile was the remedy for the fevers of malaria along the Nile, and the comfort of Peter Rabbit after a run-in with Mr. Macgregor. The demands of modern life keep this calming herb right at the top of any list of favorites.

Two similar but different plants bear the name chamomile: the perennial, ground-hugging species, sometimes called true or Roman chamomile, and a taller annual, also known as German chamomile (see page 138).

Pinch a feathery leaf or squeeze the button of a little chamomile daisy and you'll get a whiff of the clean, fruity scent, reminiscent of windfall apples. That strong aroma was used to

growing between the cracks

Plants snuggled between pavers and brick gentle a garden with the look of age. Hasten the process by slipping in starts of traffic-tolerant chamomile and thymes. Open a wedge in soil or sand between cracks with a butterknife and push in small, rooted divisions for fragrance in your footsteps.

cover up unpleasant odors in the days before indoor plumbing—strewing the fresh or dried herb on floors created an instant heavy-duty air freshener. While you may not need such strong effects, you can still appreciate the flowers' scent in potpourri or dried arrangements. Or enjoy it in the bath, in sachets, or lotions. For gleaming hair, steep a cup of dried daisies in 2 cups of water and pour over wet hair.

planting Start with young plants, set into well-drained, lean to fertile soil, in full sun.

cultivation Tolerates foot traffic if regularly watered. Transplant into lawns, to smell when passing or mowing. To propagate, lift and sever the rooted offsets spreading from the mother plant. Zones 4–9.

harvest Snip flowers when petals begin to curve backward, indicating the center has reached peak flavor. Dry, without removing petals, and store in an airtight container. Tea or other preparations made from the flowers may aggravate pollen allergies.

cichorium intybus
chicory

Chicory rewards early risers with flowers as blue as the summer sky, but as fleeting as a rainbow: by midmorning, they close up and disappear. This common, somewhat gawky roadside weed is a perennial herb prized for its root and its greens—although both are usually fancied up with an exotic name that hides their origins. The radicchio in the high-priced specialty greens section of the supermarket and the Belgian endive on your plate at that trendy eatery are both forms of chicory, bred to produce unusual coloring or reliably mild flavor.

Chicory, which is easily invited in, can be difficult to get rid of once it has settled. Adventurous cooks can cut leaves into shreds to wake up tastebuds with a hint of bitter flavor in salads or stir fries, or contrast the young, tender leaves with sweet mandarin orange segments dressed with a light vinaigrette. To grow a reasonable facsimile of "Belgian endive," cut a chicory plant to the ground in late fall, removing all leaves; set an upside-down clay pot over it, cover the drainage hole, and in spring lift the pot to harvest the blanched, emerging shoots.

Chicory arrived in America with European herbalists, who kept it as a gallstone and gout remedy. The roots, once used as a laxative, are also roasted and ground to make a coffee additive or alternative. A favorite in New Orleans and other communities of French origin, chicory "coffee" sometimes received scorn due to unscrupulous nineteenth-century merchants who sold it as true coffee, at high prices. Today, aficionados willingly pay gourmet prices for it.

Combine chicory with Queen Anne's lace and goldenrod in a meadow planting or cottage garden. Goldfinches and native sparrows seek out the seeds in fall and winter.

french quarter coffee

1 Dig roots in fall, lifting with a shovel. Cut off side shoots and trim top and tip. Wash well and slice into rounds. Dry in oven at lowest temperature, stirring occasionally.

2 When dry, increase heat to 350°F and roast for about 30 minutes, turning occasionally. Cool.

3 Grind in blender or food processor until fineness of the blend matches your usual ground coffee.

4 Brew a pot using about 1 part chicory to 3 parts coffee. Serve with croissants and raspberry jam, and imagine yourself on a balcony in New Orleans' French Quarter.

planting Easy to grow from seed, or transplant wild roots to a site in full sun, in well-drained, average to fertile soil.

cultivation Self-sows abundantly; remove unwanted seedlings with a long dandelion digger. Drought tolerant. Zones 3–11.

harvest Pick leaves young for mildest flavor. Pressed flowers are pretty in notecards and crafts; pick soon after opening, in morning. Roots can go a foot deep; dig in late summer or fall. Wash well, trim all but the meaty main section, slice and dry in oven.

Cnicus benedictus
blessed thistle

The Kudzu That Swallowed the South is a cautionary tale for gardeners: beware of inviting plants from other countries into your yard, because there's always the chance you may be nurturing a monster that will leap the garden wall. Most thistles fall into this category. Even if they don't cause big invasive problems, thistles can be a literal pain when they escape into the grass, waiting for unsuspecting bare feet.

If it weren't for these tendencies thistles would make wonderful garden plants. Their spiny foliage is dramatic in form and texture. The tufted flowers smell sweet, look good, and attract butterflies as well as goldfinches, which use the thistledown to line their nests.

The attractive spotted leaves of blessed thistle are used for stomach, liver, and gallbladder ailments, headache, fever, and flatulence. Although you may find this annual in catalogs, it's perhaps best to admire it from afar.

planting Sow seed in a sunny site, in well-drained soil.
cultivation Grow thistles of any kind only if you are vigilant about removing flowers before they set seed. Our landscapes are full of invasive plant mistakes, some unwittingly instigated by the Department of Agriculture:Japanese honeysuckle, Canada thistle, and of course the infamous kudzu.
harvest Collect leaves anytime for drying. Clip off flowerheads before they show signs of maturing to form seed puffs.

Coriandrum sativum
coriander, cilantro

Not too long ago, coriander was usually found languishing in the back of the kitchen spice shelf, the jar of whole or ground seeds pulled out only rarely to sprinkle into the occasional chicken stew. Its infrequent use was likely due to the fact that coriander is a strong-smelling herb, which causes many wrinkled noses at first sniff. The scent supposedly is the same as that of bedbugs, which you'll have to judge for yourself.

As American palates and cooks embraced the flavors of Indian, Asian, Caribbean, Thai, African, and Mexican cuisine as well as plain old meat-and-potatoes, coriander and its green leaves, known as cilantro, moved to center stage in the kitchen and herb garden. Now we know a little dab'll do us, this unique nutty, spicy, lemony, musky herb is a welcome addition. Coriander seeds warm the flavor of curries, stews, lamb, chicken, potatoes, and gingerbread and other baked goods. Cilantro carries a muskier flavor, like sage with a hint of lemon, and tastes great with veal, tomato sauces and salads, pasta, corn, and eggs. Here is reason enough to dedicate a patch to this simple-to-grow annual herb. But if you need another plus, in the spicy climes of Arabia and dank castles of the Middle Ages, coriander was used as an aphrodisiac.

The tall, open, fine-leafed plants offer clusters of understated white flowers, but tend to flop over as the seeds ripen. Edge with bright red salvia for contrast and informal stem support.

planting Sow seeds in well-drained, average soil, in full sun to part shade, in spring to midsummer. Sow thickly in rows to make early weeding easier. Grow year-round in mild-winter regions.

cultivation Make successive plantings, 2–3 weeks apart, for bountiful cilantro. Annual; all zones.

harvest Pick lower leaves anytime for fresh use; finer leaves at the top of the plant have an intense, somewhat unpleasant flavor. Unripe seeds smell bad, but they mature to pleasant lemony maturity. When plant turns brown, cut at ground level and hang over trays to let seeds drop out when they're ready. Store seed in tightly closed jars; use whole or grind before use.

a must for mexican cuisine

Cilantro is the mystery player in Mexican food, that unusual flavor you can't quite identify. Pluck leaves from stems, bruise them in your palms, and stir into chicken molé, tomatillo salsa, huevas ranchero, roasted corn, and black bean dip for authentic south-of-the-border flavor.

Crocus sativus
saffron

Harvesting this herb will make you feel like you're in a fairytale: plucking rich orange threads from inside a beautiful purple flower to make culinary magic. You'll feel even more like a fairytale character—rich old King Midas—when you consider that saffron is the world's costliest herb. That's because it takes more than a thousand flowers to yield only one ounce of saffron, and every thread must be hand-picked.

Such treasure is within easy reach of anyone blessed with a growing season that extends into September. Saffron is a crocus, and just as easy to grow as those spring harbingers that dot your garden with early cheer. But it blooms in fall. The bulb, or corm, is hardy to Zone 6, but it needs a long, hot summer extending into fall to produce the flowers you're seeking. It's worth trying, though, even if you only get flowers one year out of five; saffron crocus corms are surprisingly inexpensive, not much more than the price of regular spring bulbs.

Color is the biggest and best of saffron's attributes. Hare Krishna devotees, denizens of Mount Olympus in Greek myth, and Chinese royalty all adorned themselves with robes dyed with saffron. More practically, the blossoms also brighten the dinner plate. Just a smidgen is enough to color rice, paella, or sauces. Always be sparing with saffron, not because of its cost but because of its taste—the strong medicinal flavor is sprightly in tiny quantities but overpowering and bitter in larger amounts.

Plant saffron in its own place of honor in the herb garden, or with fall-blooming companions such as purple asters or red salvias. It forms clumps of grassy leaves when not in bloom.

saffron rice with cardamom pods

1 Heat 4 tbsp olive oil in a large saucepan. Add 2 cups basmati rice and a pinch of saffron thread about ¼ inch long. Stir over medium heat until rice is translucent. Add 4 cups water and bring to the boil.

2 Stir in 6–12 dried cardamom pods. Reduce heat to low, to keep rice at a simmer. Cover with a tight lid. Do not stir. After 15 minutes, check if water is absorbed. If not, replace lid for another 5 minutes.

3 Turn off heat and pour 1 cup frozen or fresh peas atop rice. Replace the lid and leave for 10 minutes. Before serving, stir the rice with a fork. Serves 6.

planting Plant corms in well-drained, fertile soil in full sun to light shade. If you have doubts about the length of your growing season, keep in full sun.

cultivation In cold-winter areas, mulch over winter to protect from any deep-freeze spells. Zones 6–11.

harvest Use manicure scissors to snip off at its base the deep orange, three-part "stigma" in the center of the blossom, which at first glance looks like three leggy orange threads. Do not collect the yellow stamens around the taller, more noticeable stigma. Dry saffron threads on a sheet of paper indoors. Store in a tightly lidded glass vial.

Cucumis sativus
cucumber

Just how cool is that proverbial cucumber? Cool enough to keep your face and body moisturized, to help heal an inflammation, sunburn, or a kitchen burn, and strong enough to soothe bedsores. Taken internally, this cool customer has been acclaimed for its diuretic effects in helping those with heart and kidney ailments.

Cucumbers taste best when picked before they are fully ripe, while the skin of the cuke is still entirely deep green, but herbalists let the fruit ripen. Waiting until the cukes mature means you'll get fewer per plant, because the mission of the annual vine is to produce mature fruits capable of carrying on the next generation. When you regularly pick young cucumbers, the vine keeps trying, putting out new flowers and fruits. Enjoy it both ways: pick young cukes for eating fresh or dill pickles, then let the next batch mature on the plant.

For an unlikely but appealing combination, let the vines sprawl along the ground in front of a stand of tall, tropical-looking cannas.

planting Sow seed in late spring, after soil is warm. Plant in well-drained, fertile soil in full sun.

cultivation Grow on a trellis, or use to cloak a chainlink fence. Extend mulch as vines on the ground stretch outward.

harvest For herbal use, pick when the fruits begin to turn yellow. Use them fresh. Store any extras in the vegetable bin.

a cooling facial from the garden

1 Pick one medium to large ripe cucumber. Cool in vegetable bin overnight.

2 Peel, then finely chop the cucumber in a food processor. Gently rub the juice into your skin, then slather on the pulp.

3 Lie back and enjoy the soothing facial for 10 to 15 minutes as the juice works its magic on your skin, leaving it soft and refreshed.

planting Start with a young plant; seeds are slow going. Plant in loose, rich soil in full sun to part shade, or grow in container.

cultivation Water liberally. Feed with spray-on fish emulsion or other foliar sprays. Fertilize with compost. Mulch to preserve soil moisture. Propagate by division. Zones 9–11, outdoors; grow as annual, all zones.

harvest Clip fresh leaves anytime. Before frost, harvest all leaves, cutting 2 inches above ground level. After frost, collect brown leaves as you would fresh ones. To harvest bulbs, follow a section of leaves on outside of clump to its swollen base; grasp the section above the bulb and pull upward. Cut back foliage to 4 inches; strip off tough outer leaves.

Cymbopogon citratus
lemongrass

A tall, lush fountain of fragrance, this tropical grass makes the perfect centerpiece for your herb garden. In a single season, it zooms from a puny young plant in a 3-inch starter pot to a hefty clump 3 to 4 feet tall and too big to get your arms around. That kind of record speed makes it ideal for gardens in any climate; even though freezing cold will end its life, you'll be rewarded during the growing season with an abundance of foliage for tea and other delights. Flank the entrance to a path with a pair of these plants, and in late fall you can dig up a winter's worth of sweetly edible lemongrass "bulbs" for flavoring your cooking.

Fresh lemon scent is evident as soon as you brush the grassy foliage. Use both leaves and the bulbous swellings at the base of the stems to flavor chicken, fish, vegetables, Thai spring rolls, soups, and pastas. Simmer a handful of lemongrass leaves for a mild, delicious tea, or use the brew as the base for a mixed herbal tea blend, adding peppermint or chamomile. Enjoy the clean, sharp scent, too, by chopping the leaves into potpourri, braiding them into a wreath, or scenting the bath water. Fill a handkerchief with dried lemongrass, stitch the edges closed, and lay it among your linens to give them a light fragrance. Twist a few green strappy leaves into impromptu napkin rings for al fresco dining, and your friends and family will benefit from the mosquito-deterring power of the plant. It's a close relative of citronella, which yields the pest-repellent oil that's a popular ingredient in patio candles.

In the herb garden, the upright, vertical habit of lemongrass provides strong contrast to its more relaxed neighbors. In perennial borders and other ornamental plantings, use lemongrass as you would a clump of miscanthus grass—near a garden pool, with large-leaved cannas or elephant-ears, or in the flowerbed with annuals and perennials of any kind. For a simple and beautiful combo, fill a big pot with a plant of lemongrass, red geraniums, and white cascading petunias.

storing the bounty for all-winter use

A single clump of lemongrass holds the makings for a winter's worth of tasty teas and main dishes, plus the start of next year's crop. Here's how to store the generous bounty:

1 Dry or freeze fresh green leaves, packed loosely in some zip-top plastic bags.

2 Twist frost-killed brown leaves, which are still very fragrant, into a loose coil or an open braid, so any remaining moisture can dry. Hang on the kitchen wall and slice off sections as desired.

3 Gather all the bulbs except for those in the very center of the clump. Trim the foliage back to 4 inches and store the bulbs, unbagged, in your vegetable bin.

4 Slice out remaining clump of grass and transplant into a pot to winter indoors; in mild areas, let it grow back into a full-sized clump in the garden.

Daucus carota
carrot/Queen Anne's lace

The next time you pull the common weed called Queen Anne's lace out of the soil, take a sniff of the root. Smell familiar? You've just evicted the forerunner of the plump orange carrots in your vegetable garden. The pale, skinny root in your hand is fully edible, just not as pretty or as big a mouthful as its more civilized offspring.

One of the most common wild plants of fields and roadsides, this biennial grows a ferny clump of foliage in its first year, then elongates to a 2- to 3-foot-high stem holding lacy clusters of tiny white flowers, often dotted with purple. Grow it in cottage gardens, where it will self-sow among goldenrod, coneflowers, or roses.

Queen Anne's lace and carrot roots are valued for vitamin A, noted for improved night vision. The roots, grated fresh or juiced, also soothe heartburn, and a decoction of 1 tablespoon seeds in 1 cup water helps relieve flatulence.

planting Sow seeds in spring to early fall, in a sunny site of lean to rich soil. After the first sowing, the plants will seed themselves year after year.
cultivation Control unwanted seedlings with mulch, or by prying out older plants with a dandelion digger. This is a favorite host plant for the black swallowtail butterfly—look for bold green-and-black caterpillars on the foliage. Zones 2–10.
harvest Dig roots in early fall; store extras in vegetable bin. Shake ripe seeds into paper bag for drying. Clip flowers anytime for pressing.

Digitalis purpurea
foxglove

With its charming speckled mittens strung along the stem, foxglove in bloom looks totally harmless. Don't be fooled by appearances: this innocent-looking biennial or perennial is actually one of the most potent and dangerous herbs, definitely not suitable for home experiments. The source of the well-known drug digitalis and its extract digitoxin, it makes the heart beat like a sledgehammer. That effect is just what doctors need for some heart patients, but it's too strong for the herbalist. The plant is so toxic that a small number of highly susceptible people may suffer rashes or nausea from prolonged handling.

Foxglove is welcome in the garden for its beauty and adaptable nature. Its gentle colors of white, rosy purple, soft yellow, or pale peach are easy to fit into color schemes, and its vertical lines add order and height. Plant in groups of at least three to avoid an unnatural lollipop look.

dangerous beauty
Vanity had a high price in days of old, when the cosmetic cupboard included such beautifiers as powdered lead to whiten the complexion, deadly nightshade to dilate the pupils for languid, come-hither eyes, and foxglove for the rosy cheeks and flushed bosom caused by a pounding heart and zooming blood pressure. A beautiful corpse was often the unpleasant side effect, as these poisons led to coma, stroke, and death.

snowflakes for a winter window

1 In late summer, when plants are in full bloom, cut whole flowerheads of various sizes, leaving the tiniest bit of stem.

2 Press flowerheads between pages of a phone book. Arrange the flowers carefully so that the florets are fully spread out.

3 At winter decorating time, carefully lift out the flowers, which are about to become a flurry of snowflakes on your windows. Dab a few dots of clear-drying "tacky" glue in the center of each blossom, and push against the inside pane of your windows or door.

One of the best showy flowering plants for shade, foxglove works magic along paths in a woodland garden, where its tall spires rise like pastel candlesticks among hostas and bergenia. It also enjoys sun, so use it to add old-fashioned charm to a cottage garden or traditional perennial bed. For a simple, satisfying combo, plant any color of foxglove with deep blue-purple Siberian irises and white shasta daisies, fronted with a ruff of lady's mantle. Although the deep root resents transplanting once established, it's worth gambling on moving a few pot-grown yearling plants into a large pot to make a dramatic garden centerpiece. For an unusual container composition, fill in around the leafy rosettes of a peach-colored foxglove cultivar with ruffly, deep-toned heucheras; snuggle in white and peach verbena and a plant of 'Blackie' ornamental sweet potato to drape over the pot.

planting Most cultivars bloom in their second year. Sow seeds indoors in late winter, or outside in spring to early summer, so they reach a good size by winter. Plant in sun to light shade. Keep soil well-drained with plenty of gravel and compost.

cultivation Many live only a few years, but self-sown progeny ensure a continual supply. Remove flowers before they seed to encourage side buds to bloom again. Leave a few pods to self-sow. Zones 3–9.

harvest Do not use medicinally. Wear gloves to cut and arrange bouquets if you have sensitive skin.

Echinacea spp.
purple coneflower

One of the great garden finds of recent decades, this easy-care perennial was almost unheard of among the previous generation of gardeners. An all-American wildflower of the prairies, it's blessed with abundant flowers and a long period of bloom, plus an easy-going personality. Usually untroubled by pests or diseases, it splashes gardens with color from May through frost, attracting both admiring glances and nectaring butterflies. *Echinacea purpurea* is the most popular form; the lesser-known pale coneflower (*E. pallida*) and selections with both white and purple flowers are also gaining ground.

Prized by Native Americans for treating a laundry list of ailments from snakebite to boils to open wounds, echinacea is enjoying boom times on herbal remedy counters today thanks to its reputation for minimizing allergies and boosting the immune system. Its powers, concentrated in the roots, act as what oldtimers called a "blood purifier," speeding up healing, stimulating the immune reaction, and acting as an antibiotic.

Enjoy purple coneflower in the garden as an adaptable, reliable perennial. Its rosy color is beautiful with yellow yarrow or tansy, or with pink and purple beebalm, and its deep roots resist being overwhelmed by those aggressively spreading neighbors. The leaves stay in a tidy, gradually expanding clump, so the plant is well behaved in more formal beds, too.

Because of its long bloom period, purple coneflower can ornament a bed of roses and bearded iris, then move right along to summer daylilies without pausing for breath. Ornamental grasses are natural companions from prairie days that look just as good in a garden setting. Butterflies adore the nectar-rich blossoms, and goldfinches will visit as the seedheads ripen.

making echinacea extract

1 Place washed fresh roots in bowl, and bruise with the back of a sturdy spoon. Scrape into an enamel or glass saucepan, using about 1 oz of root per 4 cups water. Bring to boil, cover, and simmer.

2 After about 15 minutes, remove the saucepan from the heat, still covered, and allow the brew to steep. When it is cool, strain out all the plant parts. Store the liquid in a glass bottle in the refrigerator.

3 Drink just 1 tablespoon of the decoction, three times a day, when the allergy season is approaching, or when you are feeling tired and run-down because of a cold coming on.

planting Easy from seed, or start with plants for bloom the same year. Sow in average to fertile, well-drained soil in full sun to part shade. Thrives in heavy clay soil.

cultivation Unusually care-free. Self-sows moderately, but extra plants are never a problem: transplant for another welcome spot of color. Zones 3–9.

harvest In late fall, dig up entire plant. Cut off largest roots for fresh use or drying. Replant rest of plant; new growth will appear in spring.

Elettaria cardamomum
cardamom

If you're a fan of curries and other Indian foods, you know the flavor of cardamom—warm, fruity, with a hint of ginger and cinnamon. In India, it grows as a shrub, but unless your climate is tropical or you have a greenhouse, this aromatic herb will only grow as big as a large houseplant.

In cold-winter climates, cardamom won't reach flowering and fruiting stage, but you can grow it as a point of interest, planted in a large pot to bring indoors in winter. Like other jungle plants, this has large leaves—up to a foot long. Its stems reach 2 feet in one summer, and up to 12 feet the next as a year-round citizen of steamy gardens. Surround it with bright red cannas or flowering ginger, or feature it on a shady patio, with pots of white impatiens at its feet.

Nibble a few seeds for fresh breath or to relieve flatulence, and slip the fragrant leaves among sweaters or linens for spicy perfume.

planting Plant roots or start with a young potted plant. Grow in rich soil in shade.

cultivation In all but Zones 9–11, grow outdoors only in summer. Supply abundant moisture, spraying foliage as well as soaking the soil at least twice weekly. Bring indoors in fall; a bathroom window makes a good home due to the high humidity levels.

harvest Should pods develop, pick them when plump and use fresh or dried. Drop whole pods into rice, curries, and other dishes, or remove the seeds inside the pods for use whole or ground.

Ephedra spp.
desert tea, ephedra

Native Americans, cowboys, covered wagon drivers, Mormons, and brothel clientele alike embraced the stimulating effects of ephedra, a native shrub of the desert Southwest that looks like nothing more than a bushy jumble of green leafless sticks. Considered a "blood purifier," it was also used as a cure for venereal disease.

Ephedra seemed like a miracle drug to modern herbalists, too, who incorporated it into over-the-counter energy boosters. As a natural pick-me-up, it was thought safe and non-habit-forming. It was especially popular with long-distance truckers and college students. Research in the 1990s, however, showed that ephedra, and especially the Chinese species ma-huang, are too risky to fool with (see box, right).

planting Order young plants from a nursery that specializes in native plants or herbs. Grow desert tea in full sun, in light, fast-draining soil. Excellent in alkaline soils.

cultivation Best in arid climates. Use in dry xeriscape gardens, accompanied by desert marigold, sagebrush, and other desert plants. Elsewhere, grow in a container filled with half sand, half soilless potting mix. Zones 6–10, depending on the particular species.

harvest Do not use medicinally. Traditionally, branches were cut and dried for use in "desert tea."

Enjoy ephedra in herb gardens or naturalistic gardens in arid climates, where its minimalist look contrasts with leafier plants. Some species grow wild from the Dakotas to Mexico, showing amazing variation, although all share the bare-stemmed look—their tiny, scale-like leaves are a water-saving adaptation. They may look like small pine trees or may hug the ground. Some have red or gray stems instead of green. The plants are male or female, with barely noticeable flowers followed by small green cones on male plants and red berries on females.

Ephedra was also used for kidney ailments, to dry up sinus problems, and to control fevers. Play it safe and simply admire it for its unusual form and long history as a helping herb.

delayed dangers

The amphetamine-like action of ephedra can cause racing heart and off-the-charts high blood pressure, leading to heart attack and stroke. Even extended use with no ill effects can't be regarded as proof that a particular user is immune to the herb's action. It can, and does, strike without warning. Efforts by the federal Food and Drug Administration appear to be heading toward a ban of ma-huang, despite its thousands of years of use in Chinese herbal medicine, and tightened controls for the less potent American species.

Plants that can kill often do their nefarious work quickly, numbing the tongue and throwing the unfortunate user into seizures, coma, or worse. Ephedra can kill outright, felling an unsuspecting user with an immediate heart attack or stroke. But its deadly action also works in sneakier ways. The elevated blood pressure caused by ephedra gradually does serious, silent damage to your heart, blood vessels, and other parts of the circulatory system. Although you may not immediately notice any alarming side effects, continued use can cause irreparable harm. Ephedra is still a component of over-the-counter diet aids, but warnings and restrictions have been attached to its use in several states.

Eupatorium purpureum
Joe Pye weed

Springtime American wildflowers like bloodroot and Virginia bluebells have been popular with gardeners for decades, but many summer and fall bloomers have only recently been invited into the garden. Perhaps that's because many later-blooming wildflowers have pushy habits, using spreading roots or myriads of self-sown seedlings to maintain their territory.

As gardeners and plant breeders get more adventurous, wildflowers of other seasons are joining their spring-blooming brethren in the garden. Among the best are members of the genus *Eupatorium*, including Joe Pye weed. All are very easy to grow, and bloom at a time when there's not much else going on.

Joe Pye isn't as well known as Johnny Appleseed, but he also spread the gospel of plants for human use. Dubbed "Joe Pye" by his white New England neighbors, the American Indian medicine man allegedly cured even typhus with the wildflower that bears his name.

Known also as queen or king of the meadow, this is one of the tallest perennials, ranging from 3 to 10 feet high. Even before it comes into its late-season glory, Joe Pye weed is a strong presence, due to its eyecatching foliage and stout, upright stems. Its leaves form whorls at intervals around the stem, like a series of widely spaced, stiff petticoats. In late summer through fall, clouds of misty mauve flowers open into huge puffs, beloved by nectar-seeking insects.

A few nearly lookalike species share similar attributes, and whatever type was handy served herbalists treating kidney and urinary problems, as well as general aches and pains. Research shows use may cause kidney and liver damage, so grow Joe Pye as ornament only.

Use it as the centerpiece of your herb garden, or plant it near water, where it often grows in the wild. In perennial beds, partner the tall species with late-blooming Maximilian sunflowers, or surround the shorter version with asters and purple coneflowers. Try it with grasses, too, with a splash of golden black-eyed Susans.

A bonus of butterflies is the payoff for growing Joe Pye weed. It is a magnet for many species, including swallowtails and monarchs on their fall migration. The fluffy flowerheads are made up of thousands of tiny florets, each holding nectar, so butterflies will feed for minutes at a time, allowing you a close-up look.

planting Start with young plants for flowers this year. Grow in wet to well-drained average to rich soil, full sun to part shade. A shorter version is 'Gateway.'

cultivation Plant where you want it to stay—the roots grow into a heavy mass, hard to pry out. May self-sow moderately. Cut back in late winter. Zones 4–9.

harvest Avoid using medicinally. Cut blossoms for bouquets anytime; cut brown seedheads after seeds disperse, for winter arrangements. Press the florets for notecards and other crafts.

Eupatorium spp.
white snakeroot, hemp agrimony, boneset

For the shady herb garden, white snakeroot (*E. rugosum*) offers drifts of white blossoms, perfect along a path or behind a bench, where it can freely colonize. Boneset (*E. perfoliatum*), another white-flowered species, was once used not to heal fractures, but to soothe the bone-deep pain of fever and flu. Both plants were also employed to treat snakebite; in some pockets of countryside, folks still say that if snakeroot is common, so are vipers.

Research indicates that eupatoriums may be injurious to health, possibly damaging the liver or kidneys. Even long ago, white snakeroot had a reputation as a poison: when eaten by cows, it caused the sometimes fatal "milk sickness," purported by some historians to have caused the death of Mrs. Lincoln.

---

planting Start with young plants, or grow from seed for bloom for the following year. Plant in sun to shade, in well-drained soil.

cultivation Best for gardens a little on the wild side; they tend to grow out of bounds quickly, either through rampant roots or self-sowing. Uproot misplaced plants by hand-pulling. Zones 2–10, depending on species.

harvest Do not use medicinally. Cut fresh flowers for bouquets anytime.

Euphorbia robbiae
spurge

The most popular euphorbia isn't to be found in most gardens—it's in millions of homes at Christmastime, given a place of honor for its big red flowers that we know as poinsettias. Look closely at other euphorbias, and you'll see the kinship: these plants have small yellow flowers atop a ruff of colored bracts that look like petals. Break a stem, and notice the milky juice that made them part of the herbal medicine chest.

Don't rub your fingers in that sap, though. It contains a substance that may cause a blistering outbreak of dermatitis. In the old days, when a thorough "cleansing" of the system was used as a last-ditch cure, various spurges were used to empty the bowels of impurities. Think Ex-Lax times 100, add a bad case of seasickness, and you have some idea of the strength of Mother Nature's "cures." And, as usual, the trouble centered around inexact dosage. Death was a frequent side effect of cure-by-spurge.

Treat it with respect, and the various spurges will make interesting ornamental plants for the garden, as well as a conversation piece. Plant them away from paths, patios, or children's play areas, to avoid accidental run-ins with the sap.

Advertisements sometimes crop up offering spurge for repelling gophers or moles. Although many species spread rapidly, burrowing animals can quickly detour around their roots. Unless you plan to cover your entire yard with spurge, its effectiveness is very questionable.

planting Start with young potted plants; most have long taproots that resent transplanting when older. Grow in well-drained lean to rich soil, in full sun to shade, depending on species.

cultivation Good for groundcover; difficult to eradicate once established. Control spread by digging or pulling up trespassers. Wear gloves and long-sleeved shirt when handling spurge. Avoid touching your gloved hand to any bare skin. Hardiness varies.

harvest Do not use for medicinal purposes. Do not cut flowers, to prevent accidental touching of the plant.

Foeniculum vulgare
fennel

Ever wonder how Roman ladies kept so slim with those bacchanals of feasting and indolence? Say hello to fennel, one of the earliest known aids for dieters. The licorice-flavored bulb, seeds, and leaves were nibbled to quiet hunger pangs of ancient Greeks at sea, Anglo-Saxons on the warpath, and body-conscious women of ease.

Fennel's flavor is strongest raw; it diminishes when cooked. Sprinkle the leaves in salads and on fish, add seeds to bread and sauces, or chop young stems for savory-sweet crunch in salads. Steam the bulb to serve with tomato or cream sauces, or eat it raw, sliced into thin pieces.

Fennel is a tall, delicate beauty with feathery leaves and slender, open form. A red-leaved form is even prettier to contrast with yellow, pink, or white flowers. The clusters of tiny flowers attract many insects, including some beneficials that will help keep garden pests under control.

planting Simple to grow from seed scattered on prepared soil. Grow in full sun, in average to fertile well-drained soil.

cultivation Self-sows abundantly. Smother excess seedlings with mulch or pull them for salads. Perennial in Zones 6–10; grow as annual, all zones.

harvest To harvest the "bulb," cut plant at soil level in fall, or when base appears sufficiently swollen. Clip leaves anytime. Shake seeds into a paper bag, or hang over cardboard trays until they fall out naturally. Use sprigs of foliage in herbal vinegars.

fennel and blue cheese hors d'oeuvres

1 Cut plant at base. Slice off tops; save these for other use. Working as with celery, pull off individual stems or "ribs" of fennel from the bulb.

2 Wash fennel stems. Trim to 4 inches, leaving an open "scoop" on one end of each piece.

3 Combine a 3-oz package of cream cheese with 1 tbsp of blue cheese. Spread onto fennel stems, as if stuffing celery.

4 Sprinkle each piece with a few caraway seeds. Garnish with a small sprig of fennel foliage. Cover with plastic wrap and store in the refrigerator until ready to serve.

easy-mow
maintenance

To help keep a
strawberry bed
vigorous, mow using a
lawnmower with the
blade set to its highest
setting (about 4 to 5
inches) in late summer,
after the fruiting
season is finished.
Rake off any debris
and watch the plants
regrow fresh and
newly invigorated.

Fragaria vesca, F. virginiana
wild strawberry

Picked at peak flavor, warmed by the sun, popped into the mouth—sweet, tiny wild strawberries are a precious commodity. They're nearly impossible for commercial growers to exploit on a large-scale level, so you'll need to grow your own to enjoy the experience.

Luckily, these appealing plants are simple to grow. Dedicate a raised bed or other area to them, or use these neat plants with their sprinkling of simple white flowers to line a path so you can simply stoop for a taste of summer. European "Fraise du bois" or Alpine strawberry (*F. vesca* 'Semperflorens') grows in tidy clumps, holding leaves upward on long stems; American

wild strawberries (*F. virginiana*) spread into colonies much faster. Both are delicious and prized by herbalists for their calming effect on nerves (whether by the pleasure of eating or by intrinsic chemical properties is open to discussion). Strawberry leaves can be made into a tea to aid digestion, diarrhea, and bellyaches.

Mashed and dabbed on the face, they have a drying effect that helps clear up oily skin and skin blemishes. A strawberry facial is also said to whiten skin and lighten freckles and age spots. If you have any strawberries to spare, experiment with the crushed fruit and juice.

Of course, wild strawberries add a special touch to desserts and salads. Scatter them atop vanilla pudding, or serve with a pitcher of heavy cream. Or you could lay a small nosegay of the long-stemmed clusters of berries on each plate.

planting Set plants 12 inches apart in rich, loose, well-drained soil. Fruiting is better when planted in sun.
cultivation These are prolific plants, with each parent sending out several new plantlets on runners during the season. Transplant these to another location to expand plantings. Cover with netting to protect from the birds. Mulch to keep the fruit clean. Zones 3–9.
harvest Pick berries when they are red and sweet. Eat fresh, dry, or freeze. Clip the leaves anytime for drying. Avoid using the leaves when fresh as they will still contain toxins.

Galium odoratum
sweet woodruff

Sniff a plant of sweet woodruff and you're likely to wonder what all the fuss is about. The only fragrance you will be able to discern smells vaguely green, certainly not anything that could be called sweet. Now, dry a leaf for about a week and try the sniff test again. Sweet indeed, with the perfumes of vanilla and new-mown hay.

Sweet woodruff spreads rapidly into a dense groundcover of deep green foliage, highlighted by sprays of starry white flowers in spring. It sulks in sun but spreads happily in shade, even in difficult areas where a heavy network of tree roots competes for moisture and nutrients. Plant it as a groundcover, accented with hostas and ferns. Fill in that forgotten deeply shaded strip beside the garage with this agreeable plant, and before you know it you'll be considering that former wasteland as a new garden.

German May wine is traditionally flavored by dried sweet woodruff, a practice dating back to the Middle Ages. After quaffing a bowl of wine, participants at May Day feasts may have slept on mattresses containing sweet woodruff—an excellent camouflage for body odors. Indeed, the sweet scent of woodruff masked a multitude of unpleasant odors: it was used to make stale rooms bearable, cover up sewage odors, and even mask the scent of a body laid out for burial.

In modern homes, sweet woodruff lends its pleasant fragrance to dried arrangements and potpourris. Use handfuls of dried foliage in herbal wreaths, or to fill a wide, shallow bowl for your hall. Show off the interesting whorled leaves, arranged in frills around the bare stem, by pressing several sprigs and arranging them in a frame as a botanical wall hanging.

planting Start with young plants; seed is well-nigh impossible to germinate. Plant in well-drained soil, in part to full shade.

cultivation Plants multiply fast by sending out running roots, from which arise new stems of greenery. Be sure to choose a location where woodruff can stay; eradicating it is painstaking work, because every small overlooked bit of the brittle roots will regrow as a new plant.

harvest You can cut the stems of foliage at any time, clipping them close to the ground with scissors. Dry before use.

a sweet scent to dream on

Perfume your pillow with the old-fashioned aroma of new-mown hay by tucking a few sprigs of dried sweet woodruff among the pillowcases in your linen closet. For a stronger scent, refreshed every time you move your head, slip a sprig of dried greenery directly inside your pillowcase. Arrange it near the top of the pillow, to avoid being disturbed like the princess and the pea. As you move your head during sleep, the pressure of the cloth against the foliage will release a light waft of perfume.

Glechoma hederacea
ground ivy, gill-over-the-ground

Chances are you may already be playing host to ground ivy. It's a common weed in many areas of North America, and often slips in by way of the roots of traded plants such as daylilies, irises, or other frequently swapped plants from friends or neighbors—unintentionally of course!

With its small scalloped-edge leaves and dainty blue flowers, plus a solid reputation as a remedy for nasal congestion, this perennial herb can be a charmer at first. But it is highly invasive, and nearly impossible to un-invite once rooted. If you already have it, celebrate its strengths and forgive its Napoleonic tendencies. After all, aren't we always looking for a pretty, indestructible groundcover that will thrive in even the worst soil? If you can, restrict its spread to beneath shrubs or among lawngrass. Weed it out when it crops up among plants of weaker constitutions, such as creeping thymes, which could be swallowed in one gulp.

planting If you have it, learn to live with it. If you don't, do not bring it into your garden.
cultivation Control by hand-weeding, making sure to remove every bit of the rooting stems. Dispose of unwanted plants in the trash, not the compost pile.
harvest Whirl half a cup of water and a handful of fresh foliage and stems, gathered anytime, in a blender or juicer to make juice. Take 1 tsp, two or three times a day, to relieve congestion.

Hamamelis virginiana
witch hazel

Witch hazel is an unusual character: it blooms in fall, long after most flowers are sleeping. In snowy areas, the incongruity of witch hazel is a complete delight when its flurry of golden flowers is topped with an icing of snow.

A common ingredient in astringents and in rubbing alcohol, witch hazel has a sharp, medicinal smell. It has been used as a gargle, to heal mouth inflammation, and as a poultice for tired or inflamed eyes, as well as for skin rashes, insect bites, and poison ivy. Commercial extract is used in aftershave preparations, sunburn lotions, and cosmetics. Because the active properties are found in the bark of this woody shrub and require special methods to extract the volatile oils, it is difficult to gather more than a very small quantity at home. Buy witch hazel water at drugstores, and plant the shrub as an item of interest rather than a source.

You can also try your luck at another old-time use of witch hazel, still employed by gifted practitioners in Appalachia and other countryfolk. The forked branches are highly flexible, which makes them ideal for use as divining rods. In the hands of a "water witcher," the forked stick is held before the body, with the single end of the branch pointing outward. When the witcher walks over a source of water, the witch hazel jerks downward, pointing to the spot where a new well should be dug. Forty-niners in the California goldrush transferred this skill to seeking out underground lodes of the gleaming metal; whether or not witch hazel was their instrument of choice is not recorded.

Witch hazel may not lead you to the mother lode, but it is definitely a garden treasure. Besides its welcome, offbeat flowers, this woody shrub or small tree has a graceful form that is most evident in winter, after the leaves drop. Other witch hazel species are equally worthy of a home in your garden. Try the Chinese variety *H. mollis*, or the so-called spring witch hazel (*H. vernalis*), which often blooms for New Year's. Modern hybrids, the offspring of a marriage between Chinese and American forms, have showier flowers and a wider color range. Underplant witch hazel with snowdrops, early crocus and other spring bulbs plus a few clumps of Virginia bluebells, which will come into bloom just as the shrub's tender new leaves appear.

planting Plant a young shrub in average to fertile, well-drained soil. American witch hazel grows best in shade, which mimics its natural woodland habitat, but it will also flourish in sun.

cultivation Water well for the first two years if rainfall is scarce. Propagate by layering. Remove suckers at ground level to keep a single trunk; hybrids may be grafted onto the root of a different species from which suckers are growing. Zones 4–9.

harvest Collect branches anytime. Clip stems of flowers for bouquets whenever they are in bloom.

soothe tired eyes

1 Clip off a branch of witch hazel at least 6 inches long, using pruners. Strip off the bark, using a paring knife. Add 2 tbsp bark to 2 cups water in a glass or enamel saucepan.

2 Cover and boil for about 10 minutes. Remove from the heat and steep, covered, for about 15 minutes. Strain out all the plant parts. Allow the liquid to cool.

3 Moisten cotton balls in the witch hazel decoction. Put your head back (or lie down) and apply to your closed eyelids for between 5 to 10 minutes.

Hepatica nobilis
hepatica

A familiar find in the wild spring woods, hepatica is just as at home in the shady herb garden. In early spring, fuzzy stems uncoil to proffer a nosegay of small purple, pink, or white starry flowers, even before the foliage appears through last fall's leaf litter. Nestle a few clumps among the exposed roots of shade trees for a cheerful greeting just when you need it most, or combine it with bloodroot, another easy-to-grow wildflower that once saw duty as a healing herb.

Now known to be toxic in large doses, it was once popular as a cure for liver problems (including the surely helpful process of "stirring a torpid liver"), blood disorders, and gall bladder pains. As a side job, hepatica tea also took on the task of soothing bronchitis. The tannins in the leathery leaves may have contributed to the alleged healing properties of the plant, but today it's best to enjoy it for ornamental value and seek help from your doctor for liver troubles.

planting Set young plants in rich, well-drained soil with a high humus content, like that found in natural woodlands beneath deciduous trees. Grows best in part to full shade.

cultivation Mulch with chopped leaves, or let fallen leaves snuggle around base. May self-sow moderately, yielding plants of various colors. Wild colonies may be centuries old. Zones 4–9.

harvest Do not use medicinally. If you can spare a few flowers, they are pretty when pressed.

Hibiscus spp.
hibiscus, mallows

Huge exotic blooms in colors that hit your eye from across the garden are the trademark of the plants commonly called hibiscus. Mostly subtropical or tropical in origin, they are widely enjoyed as seasonal potted plants in gardens across the country. Hardier sorts, such as the over-the-top 'Southern Belle' hybrids with their flowers the size of salad plates, allow northern gardeners to enjoy hibiscus as a permanent member of the garden.

Hibiscus belongs to the big Malvaceae, or mallow, family. Many plants in this large brood have been adopted by herbalists. For the home herb garden, two interesting family members you may like to sample are rose mallow (*H. moscheutos* and hybrids), for its incredible flowers, and marsh mallow (*Althaea officinalis*), for its fascinating history.

Rose mallow is a native wildflower that grows to shrub stature in wet places such as the edges of swamps, water-filled ditches, and along lakes. It adapts easily to garden life, and is a trouble-free plant that can stretch to 4 feet tall and just as wide in a single growing season. It blooms from summer through fall, with white flowers marked with a crimson eye in the "unimproved" form, or with incredible blooms in vivid reds, pinks, and snowy white, plus every streaked and splashed combination thereof. These blooms can be tricky to find companions for; try tall white phlox, or a trio of miscanthus grasses.

patio exotics

Having a tropical garden has never been easier—even if you live in Minnesota. Visit garden centers or discount stores in summer and you will find an armload of hibiscus and other lush exotic plants in bud and bloom, ready to make an instant display in your outdoor living spaces. Don't bother transplanting; simply slip the no-frills nursery pot into a classier container. Group three or more plants for that luxuriant jungle feel. Spray foliage daily with a mist nozzle on your garden hose, to supply the high humidity that tropicals crave.

Stunning summer beauty is just one reason to grow rose mallow. By rights, this plant belongs in your herb garden, where you can collect the petals to add a pleasant citrus flavor to teas.

Far more florally understated is marsh mallow, an upright perennial with velvety soft gray-green leaves and spires of small pale pink blossoms. You may recognize this herb's name from the making of "fluffernutter" sandwiches of peanut butter and marshmallow Fluff®. Although modern "marshmallow" is made from gelatin, the original type used the mucilaginous root of this herb to make the sweet confection. Root and leaves were also used to soothe sore throats and stomach ulcers. To moisturize dry hands, apply a lotion made of peeled, chopped, and boiled roots mixed with a little light olive oil.

planting Easy from seed; for bloom the same year, start with plants. Enjoys sun, average to fertile soil.
cultivation Rose and marsh mallows thrive in wet soils and coastal gardens as well as average conditions. Transplant self-sown seedlings when young. Rose mallow gets attention anywhere; quieter marsh mallow blends well with silvery herbs. Zones 3–9; winter tender species indoors.
harvest Collect rose mallow flower petals anytime. Dig marsh mallow roots in fall; use fresh or dry.

planting Start with young plants, or sow seed for bloom the following year. Plant in full sun to part shade in well-drained, lean to fertile soil.

cultivation Spreads moderately slowly by creeping roots; pull up extras. May self-sow. Plants seldom live longer than a few years; ensure a continual supply by starting new plants by division in fall. Zones 5–10.

harvest Avoid using homegrown St. John's wort internally. To soothe sunburn, mash fresh flowers in a few tbsps of vegetable oil and smooth on irritated skin.

Hypericum spp.
St. John's wort

Until the last decade, this unassuming yellow-flowered perennial got no respect in North America. A common weed of fields, roadsides, and vacant lots, its name was known only to wildflower enthusiasts, and many of them scorned it as an invader from foreign shores that competed with native plants.

Still rarely recognized along the highways and byways, its name is now familiar to millions of Americans. That's because the all-too-common malady of modern life, depression, can be alleviated by the action of the humble weed.

As savvy marketers began advertising the herb as a cure for mild depression, St. John's wort was suddenly a star in the non-prescription drug department of every discount store and pharmacy. Instead of paying high prices for popular prescription drugs, the former Prozac nation turned in droves to the inexpensive, plant-based relief of this natural cure. First documented in European studies, St. John's wort is so effective at lifting the spirits and restoring a sense of well-being that it holds a solid position among the top ten commercially made herbal products. (Photosensitivity is a common side effect: during treatment, the skin may become hypersensitive to sunlight, resulting in inflammation and dermatitis.)

To modern fans, St. John's wort seems like a miracle. To ancient aficionados, the plant was no less magical: they used it to banish evil spirits and to predict the day of death. The herb gets its name from John the Baptist, for whom the plant was said to "bleed" on the anniversary of the saint's beheading. You can try the memorial effect yourself—pinch a yellow petal and it will turn blood red. A reddish oil may also occasionally seep from the porelike glands near the edges of the leaves, especially when you crush the foliage.

St. John's wort ("wort" is an old English word meaning "plant") blooms in mid- to late summer. Place a clump near a path in the herb garden, so that you can show off its color-changing trick and inhale the sharp, piney smell of its foliage. Let it mingle with ornamental grasses, whose golden winter color will be a warm backdrop for the dark seedheads of St. John's wort.

don't try this at home

The active compounds of herbs are not always the same. Depending on the soil, the climate, the time of day, the maturity of the plant when it is picked, and a host of other variables, the volatile oils, acids, proteins, and other elements can veer from mild to potent. That's why experimenting with medicinal herbs can be a risky proposition. Brain chemistry especially is a delicate balance; don't take chances with homegrown. If you are interested in trying the effects of St. John's wort, turn to commercial products that guarantee reliable proportions of ingredients based on chemical analysis.

Hyssopus officinalis
hyssop

The pungent aroma of hyssop is a complex mix of flavors: licorice and mint with a bitter tang. To some noses, the plant smells like mothballs or Vicks salve. In cooking, the flavor stands up to robust meats and savory stews and sauces. A few snippets of its flowers or fine leaves add piquancy to salads and even fruit pies.

With such a strong medicinal scent, hyssop was a natural for home doctoring. Its foliage is known to host penicillin mold, and the oil in the plant also has antibiotic properties. Sixteenth-century herbalist John Parkinson noted that, "A decoction thereof taketh away the itching and tingling of the head, and vermin also breeding therein." Once used for treating rheumatism, whooping cough, and even leprosy, hyssop oil is no longer recommended for medicinal use either internally or externally because it causes muscle spasms and even epileptic seizures. For irregular culinary use, however, small amounts of foliage or flowers, fresh or dried, are deemed safe.

Hyssop flowers are a beautiful rich blue, and they are produced for months. Elevate a container of hyssop on an overturned clay pot as the centerpiece of a bed of herbs, where you will get a good view of the many bees, butterflies, and hummingbirds attracted to the abundant flowers. In ornamental beds and borders, mix its fine texture with plants with larger leaves and simpler flowers. For an appealing trio, plant hyssop with white petunias and yellow daylilies.

planting Sow seeds or start with young plants. Grows well in full sun to light shade, in well-drained soil. Thrives in sandy and rocky soils.

cultivation A trouble-free perennial, excellent for use in knot gardens or as a low hedge. Stems become woody with age. Propagate by cuttings of flexible green stems. Also self-sows moderately. Cut back in late winter, removing old flowerheads, to keep the plant compact. Zones 4–10.

harvest Collect flowers and new leaves anytime, to eat fresh or dry for potpourri, cookery, or flavoring tea.

Inula helenium
elecampane

Elecampane has a reputation for soothing the hacking cough of bronchitis, as well as asthma flareups and other breathing difficulties. You can try its effectiveness yourself by steeping a teaspoon of dried, crushed root in 2 cups of water and sipping it as a tea. Add honey to make it palatable; the roots are bitter. The name "scabwort" was also bestowed on this herb because of its healing effects on scabies, acne, cold sores, and other skin outbreaks.

Big, tough, and reliable, this American native holds a bouquet of fringed yellow daisies during the summer months. The stout leaves, with velvety gray undersides, may reach 2 feet long at the base of the plant. This rugged perennial is best at the back of the border or in a meadow garden, where it can show off its 4- to 6-foot height with other tall companions, such as mauve Joe Pye weed, coneflowers, and asters.

planting Sow seed, or start with young plants for flowers the first year and a root harvest the second. Plant in full sun to light shade, in fertile soil.

cultivation Choose a permanent site; removal needs persistence as new plants grow from tiny pieces of root. Grows well in clay, but to ease digging, lighten heavy soils with compost before planting. Mulch to keep moist. Propagate by slicing plantlets off base of parent, or transplant sections of root. Zones 3–9.

harvest Dig roots in late fall, after the plant is at least two years old. Dry and grind in a food processor.

Ipomoea spp.
morning glories

Only early risers get to fully appreciate the glorious silken-petaled flowers of these annual or perennial vines, which open with the sun and fade by noon. A fresh crop of blooms is produced each day, from summer through fall.

The seeds of common morning glory (*I. purpurea*) seeds were popular for a brief moment during the heyday of hippies because of their alleged hallucinogenic properties. Any such effect was due to toxins that were too dangerous for experimentation, and morning glories quickly fell out of favor as a self-administered herb. Grow the lovely flowers on a trellis to add height to your garden, and enjoy them as a nostalgic reminder of foolish youth.

A less well-known morning glory is wild potato vine, or man-of-the-earth (*I. pandurata*), which bears crimson-eyed white flowers. Below the soil, this vine produces huge edible tubers of up to 30 pounds, which were dug and roasted by native Americans. They're a close relative of the sweet potatoes (*I. batatas*, another member of the morning glory genus) that grace your table at Thanksgiving.

planting Soak seeds overnight to hasten germination. Plant directly in garden, in full sun, in well-drained lean to fertile soil; or grow in pots. Keep soil well-moistened until seeds sprout, then water weekly if rain is scarce.

cultivation Supply strings or a trellis for the vines to climb. Some species self-sow. Annuals, all zones (in areas with short growing seasons, start seeds indoors in late winter); most perennials, zones 8–11.

harvest Do not use medicinally. The thin-petaled flowers press beautifully for decorating gifts or notecards.

Laurus nobilis
sweet bay, bay laurel

Nobility is built into the Latin name of the bay tree, an evergreen from Mediterranean regions with a long and colorful history. A wreath or garland of the shining leaves signified victory with grace and honor and immediately put the wearer in high regard. The original Olympic champions were draped with bay laurel, and brave generals and inspired poets proudly wore the wreath. Of course, so did Emperor Nero and other infamous corrupt characters, who defamed the noble image of the laurel wreath.

Bay was also esteemed as powerful protection from all kinds of bad things. It was credited with warding off the plague, as well as devils and witches, who were supposed to quickly flee from the power of a bay tree. Delphic priestesses consumed mass quantities of leaves to put themselves into a hypnotic trance before making mysterious pronouncements about the future. In Greek myth, an unwilling female target of Apollo's affections took the form of a bay tree to escape the lusty god's advances. If Greek gods and evil spirits aren't troubling you, you may still find bay a comfort during lightning and thunder storms. According to the old herbalists, this noble evergreen has the power to protect anyone near it from violent acts of nature.

Our use of bay laurel today has switched from the ceremonial to the stewpot. Its aromatic leaves add personality to mild cream soups and rice dishes, and they intensify the flavor of tomato sauces and marinades. Use the leaves fresh or dried, and rub them before dropping into the pot. Keep count of the leaves you use in the recipe, so that you can be certain to remove each one before serving the food. The pointy leaf is an unpleasant surprise for diners!

Bay is a tender plant that is quickly killed by freezing cold. It grows quickly, however, and thrives in container culture. Enjoy your potted bay as a patio plant in summer, and when frost nears, move it indoors for the cold season.

planting Buy a young potted plant. Grow in full sun to partial shade, in rich, well-drained soil. Plant in a container in cold areas.

cultivation In containers, bay eventually grows to about 5 feet tall. It can reach 60 feet in the steamy heat of Florida, but elsewhere generally grows in-ground to 10 to 15 feet. Cuttings of tender green stems are difficult to root by home gardeners; use rooting hormone and be patient: it may take 6 months or longer for roots to form. Zones 8–10; wintered indoors, all zones.

harvest Clip off leaves anytime for fresh use or drying. Leaves curl as they dry; to keep them flat, hold them in place with corrugated cardboard. Cut back branches as desired to shape the plant; bay is often pruned into a formal-looking "standard," with all lower branches removed to expose the bare trunk, and the top shaped into a rounded head.

Lavandula spp.
lavenders

Everyone loves lavender—it smells sublime, it looks beautiful, it's easy to grow, and its very name evokes the romance of the Victorian era. Perfume is one of the most ancient of lavender's uses: the herb was dropped into the bathwater of ancient Rome, slipped into the bosom of a gown to delight any nose that came near, and strewn in sickrooms to freshen the air. Old-time smelling salts, sniffed by women who felt faint, combined the sweet scent of lavender oil with the sharp odor of ammonia. Lavender was also used as a moth repellent, a toothache remedy, "to comfort and dry up the moisture of a cold braine," and to ease flatulence or nausea.

Most preparations use oil distilled from blooms at their height. In full flower, the hills of France's lavender-growing countryside are cloaked in misty blue-purple, as acres of the plants await harvesting for the perfume industry.

A fondness for lavender can be the start of a lifelong collection: herb catalogs offer enough species, cultivars, and hybrids to fill every inch of the herb garden. English lavenders (*L. angustifolia*), such as 'Munstead', 'Hidcote', and dozens more, usually have darker flowers and bloom earlier than other types. 'Lavandins' (*L.* x *intermedia*) are hybrids with taller plants and larger flower spikes. Spanish, or French lavenders (*L. stoechas*) have unusual stocky heads, topped by a tuft of deep purple. 'Lady' grows fast from seed, flowering by late summer, and is often sold as an annual in multipacks.

Use fragrant lavenders with abandon throughout the garden. Edge a brick walkway, underplant roses, flank a door with potted plants, or plant them next to a garden bench and watch the butterflies and other nectar-seekers that come flocking when it blooms.

making a lavender wand

Make lavender your signature scent by tucking a lavender wand among your special stationery or in a box of all-purpose envelopes. To refresh the fragrance, just roll the beribboned head of the wand between your palms.

1 Clip about 6 to 9 fresh flowering stems of lavender, any variety, with a length of bare stem beneath the flowers.

2 Holding the bunch at the base of the flowers, bend the bare stems backward, one by one, over the flowers.

3 Arrange the bent stems so that they form a cage, with the bent bare stems on the outside and the flowers in the middle.

4 Beginning at the bend in the stems, which will be the top of the wand, weave a ⅙-inch-wide satin ribbon under and over each bare stem, continuing around the entire bundle. Use a needle to coax the ribbon into place if necessary. Lay the loose end of the ribbon along the flower spike; it will be covered as you finish wrapping.

5 Repeat, making as many rows as needed to cover the flowerheads.

6 When your weaving reaches the bottom of the flower spike, knot the ribbon around the stems and tie it with a dainty bow. The bundle of bare stems that extend from the weaving are the handle of your wand.

planting Slow from seed, except for 'Lady'; buy young plants instead. Grow in well-drained fertile soil in full sun.

cultivation In spring, trim back established plants to keep them shapely and compact. Do not cut as far back as woody stems; they will not regrow. Cut back after flowering, removing seed stalks. Propagate from cuttings of flexible young stems in spring. Most, zones 5–10; 'Lady,' all zones.

harvest Clip off flower spikes soon after opening; dry and use whole or strip flowers for potpourri and sachets. Cut foliage from spring through late summer for drying.

planting Sow seed or set young plants in full sun
to shade, in lean to fertile, well-drained soil.

cultivation Evergreen basal leaves persist in
winter, adding color to the garden. Spreads by
creeping roots and by self-sowing; hoe off
unwanted seedlings. Zone 3–10.

harvest Do not use medicinally. Avoid contact
with bare skin.

Leonurus cardiaca
motherwort

A common plant of roadsides and woods' edges in parts of North America, motherwort looks something like a delphinium plant out of bloom. At flowering time, however, the difference is distinct: instead of delphinium's tall spire of beautiful blue flowers, motherwort bears tiny, pale purple or white flowers tucked against the stem at the upper leaves.

Although its name leads us to believe the herb was useful for childbirth, this mother's helper was named for easing the symptoms of menopause. An infusion of 1 teaspoon leaves steeped in half a cup of water was swallowed in a dosage of "one mouthful" per day to alleviate hot flushes, as well as to reduce the pains of arthritis, sciatica, and neuralgia. The word *cardiaca* in the herb's botanical name alludes to its long-ago use as a heart stimulant, a good reason to grow the plant only as a curiosity in the modern herb garden.

Use motherwort as a background plant, where its 3-foot height and toothed leaves can serve as a cool green backdrop for silvery herbs or bright-flowered plants. Brushing bare skin against the foliage may result in dermatitis in some susceptible individuals; wear long sleeves and gloves when handling the plant, to be on the safe side. Its flowers are highly attractive to bees, another good reason to keep the plant away from the path of traffic.

Liatris spicata
blazing star

Like purple coneflower, blazing star is a prairie native that has only recently become a fixture in American gardens. Its bright purple-pink fuzzy spikes aren't as familiar yet as the rosy daisies of coneflowers, but they are quickly gaining ground, thanks to their hardiness, adaptability, and long-lasting flowers. Butterfly enthusiasts quickly learned that blazing star works like a magnet for the stunning swallowtails of summer.

Blazing star was prized by early herbal practitioners because the tuberous roots were used as an attempted cure for venereal diseases, which ran through the ranks of explorers, settlers, and native Americans alike.

Modern drugs have made blazing star treatments obsolete, but the flowers are still welcome for their bright dash of summer color. The most commonly grown species, *L. spicata*, is a tall, showy plant, also called gayfeather for its cheerful purple spikes. Plant it with prairie companions, such as purple coneflowers and goldenrod, for vivid summer color.

planting Most economical from bulbs, planted in spring or fall. Or buy young potted plants. Set in full sun, in fertile, well-drained soil.

cultivation Drought tolerant. Long bloom period. Propagate by digging up clump in early spring and separating bulbs. Zones 2–10.

harvest Not recommended for medicinal use. Cut fresh flowers anytime for long-lasting bouquets.

sore throat or snakebite

Blazing star is one of many herbs that were used for a variety of unrelated ailments. Settlers with a sore throat could gargle with the same decoction they swallowed to treat more serious symptoms of the private parts. Scaly blazing star (*L. squarrosa*) served as first aid for rattlesnake bites; after the venom was sucked out of the wound, the root was applied to finish drawing out the poison.

Linum spp.
flax

One of the oldest crops in cultivation, flax provided the wrappings for Egyptian mummies, the sails for Roman ships, and the oil for Italian master painters. The burial shroud of Turin, whose provenance is still in dispute, is made of linen produced from flax. So are the translucent pages of old Bibles, as well as early cigarette papers and modern high-quality stationery.

The flax plant has delicacy written all over it, from its ethereal sky-blue blossoms that tremble with every slight shift of breeze, to its thin, fine stems and tiny needle-like leaves. Behind that graceful personality, though, is one tough customer. The tissue-thin linen blouses and soft, thick linen pants we know today are a far cry from hopsacking and linsey-woolsey, which were woven from homegrown flax and prepared by hand. New clothes were more torture than delight in those days: they required a long breaking-in period before they stopped chafing.

weight-loss wonder or diet dud?

Flax seeds enjoyed a boomlet of popularity in recent years as a much-touted aid to losing weight. Most customers didn't come back for a refill, however, because the way in which the pounds were shed had more to do with oil's laxative properties than with some magical fat-melting ingredient. Once used as a constipation cure to rid the bowels of the "poisons" that supposedly caused various illnesses, flax seeds swell up in the intestines as they absorb water. Before long, the innocent user is indeed losing ounces and pounds, but not in the hoped-for manner.

Oil-rich flax seeds fed oxen, cattle, and humans alike for thousands of years. Today, commercially grown seeds of annual flax (*L. usitatissimum*) are used for linseed oil, and in animal feeds and birdseed mixes—they're a favorite of finches.

To the herbalist, flax was indispensable. A tea made from the gluey crushed seeds cured coughs and colds, and supposedly halted urinary infections. Unfortunately, an overdose might also cause staggering, gasping for breath, and eventual paralysis, due to toxic compounds in them. A safer treatment is to grind and boil the seeds for a poultice for burns and skin sores.

Plant three or more clumps together in the herb garden or in flower beds, to increase the impact of their willowy stems and dainty flowers. The blossoms fade by late morning, but a new batch of blue will open the next day. The delicate color and texture is beautiful with bold flowers, such as painted daisies, poppies, or bearded iris.

planting Easy from seed, or buy young plants. Grow in full sun, in well-drained, average to rich soil.

cultivation Self-sows moderately. Learn to recognize seedlings so you may transplant them. Zones 4–9.

harvest Gather only fully ripe seeds; unripe seeds are high in toxins. Clip seedheads and shake the shiny brown seeds into a tray to dry for a week or so. More than 700 pounds of fiber can be reaped from a single acre of the plants, which are pulled up and soaked for weeks to rot the stems off the threads.

Matricaria recutita
German chamomile

You'll want to dedicate a patch of your herb garden to German chamomile, so that you have bountiful makings for tea and potpourri within easy gathering reach. But do allow the plants to self-sow and snuggle into unexpected corners, too. Scatter chamomile seeds beneath roses for a charming lace collar all summer long, or grow a mixed bed of edible flowers, by sprinkling seeds of chamomile, borage, and calendula in the same patch of prepared soil.

Both German chamomile and perennial chamomile (*Chamaemelum nobile*, see pages 100–101) are well known as calming herbs, and that reputation includes muscle tightness as well as nervous anxiety. Brew the flowers into a strong tea and add to a hot bath for a relaxing soak. The blossoms have antiseptic properties; gargle with cold tea to soothe mouth ulcers or sore throat. To make blond hair shine, steep 2 cups of blossoms in 2 quarts of boiling water for 30 minutes; strain, cool, and pour slowly over hair. If you are allergic to pollen, you may experience symptoms from such treatments.

grow a gift of sleepytime tea

The light apple scent, warm liquid, and calming action of the herb make chamomile tea the ideal before-bed beverage. The dried blossoms look great packed loosely into a sealed glass jar. Add a pretty label with the recipe: Put 1 to 2 tsp chamomile flowerheads in a teaball in a cup. Fill with boiling water. Steep for a few minutes, then remove the teaball and add honey to taste.

planting Scatter seed in fall or spring on prepared soil. Grow in full sun, in well-drained soil.
cultivation Make successive sowings every few weeks for a continual supply. Annual; all zones.
harvest Clip off flowers when fully open, for fresh use or drying. Store in tightly sealed glass jars.

Melissa officinalis
lemon balm

The clean, fresh lemon scent of this perennial is wonderful in teas and a pleasure to sniff as you stroll the garden. But too much of a good thing can quickly become the case, as it spreads by creeping roots and has a habit of self-sowing to the point of weediness. Strays are easy to uproot or smother with mulch when very young, though, so don't let the plant's profligacy deter you from trying it. The flowers are also manna to bees.

Lemon is a popular scent in aromatherapy, reputed to clear the mind, sharpen memory, and relieve headaches and depression. Try it yourself by bruising and inhaling the aroma of a leafy stem. Lemon balm's herbal reputation carried things a few steps further: the plant was said to cure the effects of mad dog bites, prevent baldness, and even restore a "crooked neck."

Grow it in its own raised bed. Forms with golden or variegated foliage are also available.

custom tea blends

Lemon balm produces so much foliage, you can easily harvest a season's supply from a single plant with three successive cuttings. Dried leaves make an excellent, mild lemony base for hot or iced teas. Combine it with one or more of the following to create your own special tea blends:

anise seeds, basil, beebalm, chamomile, cardomom pod, fennel seeds, hibiscus petals, peppermint, rose hips

planting Sow seed, or start with young plants. Grow in full sun to shade, in well-drained soil. Plants may become floppy in shade; cut back as needed to keep them compact.

cultivation Slow down self-sowing by cutting plant halfway back after flowering, before seeds form. Uproot stragglers by hand. Zones 4–10.

harvest Fresh leaves make the most flavorful tea. Gather before flowers open. For large quantities, cut entire plant at ground level. Air dry on screens for winter use. Add stronger herbs for more flavor.

Mentha x *piperita*
peppermint

The mints are a large family of plants that have been treasured for millennia for their medicinal properties. Several species carry scents so familiar we can identify them with our eyes closed. Most familiar is peppermint. Rub a leaf and you'll immediately recognize the pungent aroma of menthol: the scent of Christmas candy canes and breath-freshening after-dinner mints.

Peppermint tea is one of the best remedies for an upset stomach. Chewing a few fresh leaves also relieves mild indigestion or flatulence. The herb is also said to relieve insomnia, and it may help soothe migraines. Chopped and tied in cheesecloth, the fresh leaves can be dropped into the bath to quiet the itch of winter-dry skin.

For a refresher of a different sort, try a homemade mint julep to celebrate Kentucky Derby Day. Use the back of a spoon to crush 6 to 10 fresh peppermint leaves against the side of a bowl. Add 1 jigger of bourbon and 1 tablespoon quick-dissolving sugar; stir well. Fill serving glass with crushed ice; strain bourbon/mint mixture into the ice. Churn up and down with a metal spoon until thoroughly mixed. Top off with more crushed ice, top with a fresh sprig, and add a straw for sipping as you watch the race.

Peppermint is grown commercially to flavor chewing gum, candy, and other products. In the Pacific Northwest, the fields can be recognized from a distance by their beautiful deep red color against a backdrop of blue mountains.

planting Mints hybridize readily, so start with young plants that come from a reliable source, and sniff-test them first. Plant in well-drained to moist soil, in full sun to shade.

cultivation Peppermint spreads rampantly (see page 142 for control suggestions). If the patch is large, mow it with the blade set at its highest setting in early summer for a fresh flush of compact growth. Hand-pull carefully, any bits of underground stems will quickly sprout anew. Zones 5–10.

harvest Collect foliage anytime for use fresh or dried. To harvest large amounts, clip off plants at ground level before bloom time.

Mentha pulegium
pennyroyal

Ground-hugging pennyroyal has a different look from most common mints. Its neat, shining leaves form a thick carpet as the plant expands, topped by stems of lavender-blue flowers in late summer. It's easier to keep in bounds than the taller, more aggressive mints; try it as an underplanting for roses, where its strong scent may help repel insect pests. The thick green carpet is also attractive when it creeps among rocks or stepping stones.

Sometimes known as English pennyroyal, this herb smells somewhat like peppermint, with a hotter, spicier undertone. American pennyroyal (*Hedeoma pulegioides*) shares the signature aroma, but is an upright, branching annual.

Neither species is edible. In fact, the oil in pennyroyal is a deadly toxin that can destroy the kidneys when taken internally. The herb was occasionally administered to induce abortion, but often proved deadly to the mother as well as the baby. Keep these plants out of your mint patch, where they may be mistakenly picked for internal use, and away from other edible plants.

Pennyroyal does have its useful side. Its odor repels insects, especially ants. If ants climb the post of your hummingbird nectar feeder, plant pennyroyal around its base to help deter them.

planting Buy young plants; English pennyroyal is slow to start from seed. Grow American pennyroyal from seed. Both do best in well-drained soil in full sun.

cultivation Water regularly if rains are scarce. Propagate by division. Zones 5–10; American pennyroyal, all zones.

harvest Do not use internally. Pick fresh leaves anytime to crush against insect stings or bites.

deodorize your fingertips

Preparing fish, chopping onions, peeling garlic, or smoking cigarettes can leave your fingers with a tattletale aroma. To magically remove unpleasant odors from your fingers, rub a leaf of a strong-smelling mint between them until the odor is gone. Pennyroyal, peppermint, and spearmint are particularly fast-acting deodorants. If you use pennyroyal, be sure to wash your hands with soap and water afterward.

Mentha spicata
spearmint

keeping mints in check

Mints are notorious for rampant spreading. To keep your herb garden from being swallowed alive, try these tricks:

1 Give mints an area where they can freely roam, perhaps a hard-to-mow slope or the strip of soil between street and sidewalk.

2 For a small mint patch, cut out the bottom of a plastic bucket and bury it so the top rim extends 3 inches above ground. Plant mint inside.

3 Paint a child's stiff plastic swimming pool deep green-black. Fill two-thirds deep with soil and plant inside.

4 Grow mints in water: a few stems in a big jar of water will root quickly, and grow for months.

This grows wild across America, especially along streams where it spreads into thick, fragrant beds. These plants are escapees from long-ago gardens, where the herb was imported with the first waves of European settlers.

The scent is instantly recognizable to anyone who has ever unwrapped a stick of spearmint-flavored chewing gum. In herbal lore, its uses are similar to those for peppermint: it works as a stomach soother, to ease indigestion, nausea, and heartburn. Simmer a handful of fresh, bruised leaves for tea, or nibble on the greenery. It's also a great remedy for bad breath.

Less intense than peppermint, this is a favorite in cooking. It's traditionally served with spring lamb, and can also be used for cold mint juleps, and even jelly; add some fresh leafy stems to a mild apple jelly in the last minutes of cooking.

planting Start with young plants from a reputable source; the strength of scent in seed-grown plants varies widely. Plant in sun to shade, wet to dry soil.

cultivation Controlling the plants is the trickiest part. Uproot strays ruthlessly. Zones 5–10.

harvest Gather foliage anytime. For large amounts to dry, cut them at ground level before flowering time.

Monarda spp.
beebalm

Want hummingbirds in your garden? Plant bright red beebalm and they will come. The zippy little birds simply can't resist the nectar-filled flowerheads. Other colors of beebalm also satisfy their sweet tooth, but red is key to tempting them to your yard for the first time.

Beebalm has odd-looking flowers, but if you take a close look, you'll see why they're perfect for hummingbirds. Each shaggy head is actually a cluster of many tubular flowers, each facing outward so that it is perfectly positioned for a hovering bird to sip from. The foliage below the flowers is what gives this herb its alternate name of bergamot: it has a light, citrusy scent like that of bergamot oranges.

A member of the mint family, as you can tell from the square stems, beebalm makes delicious tea that was first brewed by Oswego Indians living near Lake Ontario, New York. Centuries later, when hot-headed colonists ditched crates of imported and highly taxed black tea into Boston Harbor during their Tea Party protest, readily available beebalm or "Oswego tea" became the drink of choice. It can quiet an upset stomach and relieve flatulence and nausea. Oswego tea was also quaffed to soothe a cough or sore throat, and to relieve menstrual cramps.

Beebalm is an all-American plant, with several species, all of which can be used for making tea. *Monarda didyma* blooms red in the wild, although plant breeders have developed a further range of colors from white to purple; it is often found near water or in shady woods although it thrives in sunny gardens, too. Mauve *M. fistulosa* is native to dry open fields, where it blooms in late summer with goldenrod and asters. All beebalms are well suited to meadow gardens, where they can spread at will, or to flowerbeds, where they require a firm hand to keep in bounds. Partner beebalm with purple coneflowers, shasta daisies, and yarrow, or let it mingle with daylilies in shades of pink and pale yellow. Beebalm flowers are edible; pull them apart and toss in salads, or dry them for long-lasting color in potpourri. Chop young leaves and add to sliced strawberries or melon for a hint of orange flavor.

planting Start with young plants; slow to start from seed; modern colors do not come true from seed. Plant *M. didyma* in full sun to shade, in average to wet soil. Plant *M. fistulosa* in sun, in dry to average-moisture soil.

cultivation Beebalm is a mint, and it spreads fast by underground stems. Hand-pull strays to keep in bounds. Propagate by division. Zones 4–10.

harvest Cut foliage anytime for use fresh or dried; for large amounts, cut entire plant at base before flowering time. Cut flowers soon after opening for bouquets, for fresh culinary use, or for dried arrangements and potpourri.

homegrown acne treatment

To dry up pimples, boils, and other skin outbreaks, American natives and early settlers turned to wild bergamot (*M. fistulosa*). The leaves of beebalm (*M. didyma*) may have the same effect, as both contain an oil that acts as a germ-killer, fighting fungi and bacteria.

Boil a cup of fresh leaves in enough water to cover, for about 5 minutes. Cool slightly, then apply wet leaves to irritated skin for about 10 minutes.

planting Sow seeds in full sun to shade, and in loose, rich, humusy soil.

cultivation Self-sows. Clip the flowers after they fade to control, if desired, or smother any errant seedlings with mulch. Zones 5–10.

harvest Cut foliage anytime for use fresh or dried. Dig roots in fall. Shake seedheads into trays for a week of further drying.

Myrrhis odorata
sweet cicely

Looking very much like a fern when not in bloom, sweet cicely forms a clump of feathery green leaves that stay fresh through most of winter. Also known as licorice root, this perennial herb holds the sweet scent of anise in its leaves, stems, and seeds, as well as its fleshy, fingerlike taproots. Rub a leaf and you will quickly smell the trademark aroma. (That sniff test is also a good way to check the plant's identity: both poisonous wild hemlock and harmless Queen Anne's lace can look similar to this herb.)

Two similar-looking plants share the name and attributes of sweet cicely. *M. odorata* is European, and *Osmorhiza longistylis* American. Use the foliage, root, or seeds to sweeten teas or flavor baked goods, soups, fish, and potatoes.

Nasturtium officinale
watercress

The deep green leaves and crunchy stems of this aquatic perennial add a peppery bite to salads, and are great in a chicken-stock potato soup. It is rich in vitamin C, iron, and iodine, and before vitamin C was available year-round, watercress was eaten to treat scurvy. Its juice was used as an expectorant, to clear the lungs, and was even rubbed on scalps in the hope of restoring hair.

planting Easiest to start by rooting a few fresh stems. Strip the lower leaves and insert stems in loose, moist soil. Keep soil well watered during growing season. A spot near to a pool or faucet is ideal.

cultivation Mulch to keep moist and clean. Cabbage butterflies may lay eggs on them. All zones.

harvest Cut stems of leaves before they form flower buds, when the flavor turns bitter. Use fresh.

salad in a saucer

A 3-inch-deep plastic plant saucer makes a good home for watercress, and saves on watering chores. Pour in ½ inch soilless peat-based potting mix and fill with water. Poke in a few stems; they quickly grow aquatic roots and will produce foliage above the water.

Nepeta cataria
catnip

If Kitty is your best friend, you'll definitely want to plant this herb to send her into fits of delight. Your planting may look a little battered after it endures the rubbing and rolling of feline ecstasy, but this hardy perennial herb will quickly spring back, ready for another round. Interestingly, some cats seem entirely unmoved by catnip. Instead of acting intoxicated, they ignore the plant. Researchers theorize that some cats are genetically unsusceptible to nepetalactone, the chemical in catnip and related hybrid catmint (*Nepeta* x *faassenii*) that triggers the reaction.

Catnip is a coarse, bushy, self-sowing perennial that can quickly turn weedy. If you want to make a big brood of catnip mice for gifts, this is a good trait. Grow it in a raised bed or cottage garden, where it can self-sow at will.

For a more controlled garden, try catmint (see photo, right), which does not self-sow. Besides being more compact, it yields hazy billows of blue-purple flowers that look great with roses, iris, poppies, and other perennials.

planting Start with young plants, or ask a friend for a few cuttings; they root in about a week. Grow in sun to shade, in almost any soil.

cultivation Allow space around the plant so that feline friends have easy access. Zones 4–10.

harvest Clip entire plant at base before flowering, to dry for crafts or minty tea. Cut catmint flowers soon after they open for fresh bouquets or drying.

Ocimum spp.
basil

Your first armload of homegrown basil will make you feel like a blue-ribbon gardener. Basil is heady stuff—highly aromatic, super prolific, and as simple to grow as marigolds. For a $2 investment in a packet of basil seeds, you can harvest about a year's supply of this first-rate culinary herb. Bring on the tomatoes, the mozzarella, the chicken, the pasta, the shrimp: with basil in your garden, your cooking is about to take an inspired leap.

Sweet basil (*Ocimum basilicum*) is the name for the traditionally scented annual herb. It has a strong, sharp aroma with a heavy hint of licorice and a spicy warmth—a unique flavor that most folks enjoy from their first bite. Slice the leaves onto a frozen pizza, whirr them into pesto, simmer them in sauces. Almost any Italian dish tastes better with a little basil. Because the flavor is so dominating, however, use basil with a light touch until you know the preferences of your friends' and family's palate.

The popularity of plain old basil has inspired plenty of "new and improved" versions with fancy leaves or unusual scents, plus a host of rediscovered exotic basils, including Thai, African, and clove-scented varieties. Sampling the many types of basil available is a fun way to expand your sensibilities, but be sure to leave enough room for the regular all-purpose variety alongside the curly basil, the cinnamon basil, the ruffled basil, and the miniature basil. The extra-large leaves of 'Lettuce Leaf' basil will save you time de-stemming when you're ready to mix up a batch of pesto.

Grow basils either in their own beds or as decorative accents or edgings. 'Spicy Globe' basil, which forms a tidy ball of small leaves, lends a formal attitude when evenly spaced. The dramatic color of 'Purple Ruffles' or smooth-leaved purple basil is striking next to yellowish green lemon basil, or with garden flowers as an ornamental. One of the best ways to show off a collection or prized specimen of basil is in a container. Elevate the pot by setting it on top of another, overturned pot to give it even more visual drawing power.

quick and easy pesto, and variations

Basic Mix 2 cups fresh basil leaves, 3 cloves garlic, ¼ cup pine nuts, and 1 cup olive oil in a blender. Process until a thick paste. Toss with hot pasta, spread on toast, dab on pizza, or use as a dressing for sandwiches. Freeze extra in ice cube tray, then unmold and put in zip-top freezer bags.

Cheesy Add ½ cup Parmesan and ¼ cup Romano or Asiago cheese to basic recipe. Great on English muffins with tomato, breaded eggplant, and poached scallops.

Walnut Substitute English walnuts for pine nuts in basic recipe. Tasty with cheese-filled ravioli or Hungarian pierogies

(potato dumplings). Or split a loaf of French bread, dab with pesto and chèvre cheese, and broil until toasted and the cheese is melted.

Lemon Add juice of 1 large or 2 small lemons to basic recipe. Great with fish or chicken dishes, or serve with hard-boiled eggs and grilled chicken salad for an easy brunch.

planting All basils are easy and fast to grow from seed, although multipacks of plants are also available. Plant in well-drained, average to fertile soil, in full sun.

cultivation Clip back every two to three weeks to encourage new leafy growth and delay flowering. Learn to recognize seedlings; some basils self-sow. Annual; all zones.

harvest Cut leafy stems or pick individual leaves anytime; the flavor is best before the flowers open. For large quantities, cut the entire plant at ground level. In cold areas, cut basil at ground level when frost threatens.

Oenothera biennis
evening primrose

This tall biennial is rarely planted in American gardens, unless its seeds are included in a packet of mixed wildflowers. Yet it is one of the most noteworthy herbs, with science backing many of its claims; it is also a charming easy-care flower for meadows and cottage gardens. The flowers open while you watch, with a snap and release of light, sweet perfume—this magical show takes place around sunset from mid- to late summer. Oil extracted from its seeds has been used with great success to alleviate symptoms of premenstrual tension, and trials have seen many eczema sufferers experience improvement. The oil may also alleviate hangovers, depression, arthritis, obesity, and acne, and is being studied for treatment of multiple sclerosis. The wonder-working substance is gamma-linolenic acid (GLA), also found in borage seed. Stay tuned for further developments in research and future products introduced to the public.

planting Easy from seed. Forms a rosette of leaves the first year and blooms the next. Plant in sun to part shade, in well-drained, lean to fertile soil.

cultivation Self-sows moderately. Flowers open late evening and close by mid-morning. Look for visiting moths soon after the flowers open. Zones 4–10.

harvest Not recommended for home medicinal use. Enjoy it in the garden with purple coneflower, asters, and other summer-into-fall flowers.

Origanum majorana
marjoram

Lighter in flavor than spicy oregano, marjoram is the delicate cousin of that hearty Italian-cooking staple. Beware of mislabeled plants; confusion reigns among the oregano clan. Although marjoram is frost-tender, it grows rapidly, and forms a large, sprawling mound in a single season. The flowers attract butterflies and other nectar-seeking insects, among them a multitude of wasps and other beneficial insects that will help control pests in other parts of your garden.

Grow marjoram along rock walls, where it can spill among the stones, or let it trespass onto brick pathways, where its lively scent will be released by the occasional tread of passersby.

Use marjoram as you would oregano: in Italian cooking, with beef or chicken, in soups and sauces, or on grilled vegetables. Mash a few leaves with butter and use for corn on the cob or baked potatoes. It also adds a piquant note to potpourri and sachets, without smelling like you accidentally sprinkled on the pizza topping.

planting Buy young plants from a reputable source; sniff before you buy if possible. Plant in light, very well-drained soil of lean to average fertility. Also thrives in containers.

cultivation Propagate by division. In cold areas, start new plants in late summer, to winter indoors on a windowsill. Zones 9–10; grow as annual, all zones.

harvest Cut leafy stems anytime. Collect large amounts before they bloom, for use fresh or dried.

Origanum vulgare
Greek oregano

Travel the picturesque byways of New England in late summer and you'll see oregano in full glorious bloom, creating a haze of rosy purple along the roadside like an American version of the Scottish moors. Like many herbs, oregano escaped from gardens of long ago, from which it made the leap to other open, well-drained homesites. A member of the mint family, oregano spreads nearly as fast as its cousins, although it is much easier to control because its rooting stems travel along the top of the ground, where they are easy to pull up by the handful.

Do keep a big patch of oregano in your herb garden, because you'll want plenty to use fresh and dried. The pungent, spicy flavor is a key note in tomato sauces, pizza toppings, Italian beef stews, and many other dishes. Try it with grilled vegetables, potatoes, in scrambled eggs or bean dip, or mixed into cream cheese for bagels.

take the sniff test before buying

Oregano plants vary widely in their smell and flavor—some have barely any scent at all and others are strong enough to make your mouth water for spaghetti. Seed-grown plants are usually insipid; look for plants grown from cuttings or divisions of strong-smelling parents. If possible, always sniff before you buy. Even young plants will release the strong, characteristic odor of oregano when you bruise a leaf.

planting Buy young plants from a reputable source; sniff before buying. Site in full sun, in well-drained soil, low to average fertility.

cultivation Plants retain some foliage during winter. Golden oregano has lovely warm-colored foliage year-round. Zones 5–10.

harvest Clip foliage anytime for use fresh or dried. Harvest large amounts before plants bloom. Snip flowers anytime for bouquets, dried arrangements, or for pressing.

Panax quinquefolius
ginseng

plant for the future

Ginseng is a long-term investment, not in money but in time. The roots take at least 7 years to develop to usable size, and older is even better. Because the desired root chemicals are diluted by faster growth, it won't help to douse it with fertilizer.

Pick a shady, undisturbed site— under sugar maples is ginseng's preferred habitat in the wild—and plant a small patch for the future. Prepare soil by digging in large amounts of chopped leaves composted until they crumble into loose, black soil-like material: the same stuff you find in the forests where ginseng grows. Plant young roots (or seeds), and do not disturb until next decade. Let fall leaves lie in place.

Once a common wildflower of much of the eastern half of North America, ginseng today is rarely encountered in the wild. Greed is the reason for the plant's decline. Its healing roots were sought not only by countryfolk, but later by speculators who combed the forests and sold the plants at extremely high prices for export to the Chinese market. Ginseng grows very slowly, needing about seven years to grow marketable roots, so unscrupulous "sang" collectors soon dug themselves right out of a job.

The long, fleshy ginseng root—often shaped like a crude human figure—is the powerful part of the plant. Esteemed as an aphrodisiac and all-around health enhancer, ginseng is held to be as vital to mental acuity as to physical well-being.

Grow ginseng in a shady garden, among ferns and wildflowers such as mayapple, wild blue phlox, and bloodroot. In fall, its shiny red berries add a flash of color; pluck off a ripe berry and you'll see it is shaped like a plump, puffed heart.

planting Buy young plants from a nursery that propagates their own stock and, hence, does not collect it from the wild. Plant in moist, humusy soil, in the shade.
cultivation Mulch with chopped leaves to keep the soil moist. Do not cultivate nearby, to avoid disturbing the root.
harvest Should your ginseng crop mature to the point you can spare a plant, dig roots in late fall.

Papaver spp.
poppies

Beautiful, ruffled poppies are renowned for the stress-reducing effects of some species—most notably, the opium poppy (*P. somniferum*), a lovely annual with gray-green leaves and blooms in hues of pink, red, and purple. Naturally, you won't be growing them for nefarious purposes, but you can indulge a passion for poppies by growing any of the perennial or annual types.

The red poppies of Flanders fields (*P. rhoeas*) immortalized in fund-raising paper flowers sold by veterans, are simple to grow from seed. Both field and opium poppies (available in narcotic-reduced strains) produce copious amounts of tiny black seeds, which make a tasty topping for muffins and other baked goodies, although they may show up on sensitive drug tests.

Plant poppies in a large patch to enjoy a sweep of silken-petaled color. Or scatter seed in a cottage garden or informal flower bed, where they mingle happily with columbines, daisies, irises, and other early summer flowers.

planting Sow seed for annuals directly in garden; seedlings are nearly impossible to transplant. Grow in full sun, in well-drained, fertile soil.
cultivation Annuals self-sow. For lasting poppies, try perennial Orientals; propagate by root cuttings. Annuals, all zones; perennials, Zones 3–10.
harvest Pick almost-open buds for display; sear stem ends. Use seed capsules in dried arrangements. Shake ripe seeds into paper bag for culinary use.

Pelargonium spp.
scented geraniums

You can make an entire herb garden from just scented geraniums. Dozens of cultivars with mouth-watering aromas and a delicious variety of form and foliage make it an exercise in self-restraint to limit yourself to just two or three. Luckily, it's easy to fit these agreeable tender perennials into the garden: they stay in tidy, branching clumps, so you can use them as accents, plant them as edgings, or grow them in windowboxes or containers to showcase a single specimen or display a whole range.

Start your collection with the classic rose geranium, whose lobed leaves lend a pleasing flowery scent to cakes and teas. Add the extra-curly foliage of lemon geranium, a smaller plant with a neat, upright habit. Make room, too, for apple geranium, a relaxed plant, perfect at the edge of a large pot, where its soft gray, rounded leaves and delicate white flowers can spill over the rim. Then fill in any gaps with your favorite scents: chocolate, geranium, nutmeg, orange, coconut, peppermint, eucalyptus, and just about any other aroma you can think of. All are great for flavoring desserts and drinks, and scenting cosmetics; the leaves themselves are not eaten.

Unlike traditional red windowbox geraniums, the flowers of scented geraniums take a backseat to the foliage. There is incredible variety of leaf shape and size, from round leaves the size of a thumbnail to bold lobed leaves almost as big as your hand. Many display beautiful variegation, with crisp white margins or snow-speckled foliage. Chocolate peppermint offers wide green leaves splashed with brownish purple. Several types have velvety gray leaves, with and without creamy trim. Oakleaf, which has a unique spicy scent, bears leaves shaped like that of a white oak. Flowers are usually pink or white, with a delicate, airy look.

apple geranium afterbath soother

1 Bruise 6 to 10 apple geranium leaves. Stir into 1 cup extra-light olive oil, in a small pan.

2 Set on low or warm heat, stirring frequently to release oil from the leaves into the mixture.

3 When oil is fragrant and very warm to the touch, remove pan from heat, cover, and cool. Strain and funnel into a bottle with a squeeze top. After a shower or bath, smooth the oil sparingly on skin.

planting Buy young plants; scented geraniums are started from cuttings. Plant in full sun to part shade, in well-drained fertile soil.

cultivation Pinch the plants to encourage more compact growth. In cold areas, start cuttings in midsummer to winter over indoors. Zones 9–10; wintered indoors, all zones.

harvest Clip individual leaves or sprigs anytime. Cut flowers for pressing soon after opening.

Perilla frutescens
perilla

Ruffly, aromatic perilla is an Asian herb that often turns up on plates of Chinese, Korean, and Japanese food. Also known as shiso, it can be eaten in all stages of growth. When sprouting, it garnishes food with spicy red or green color. The leaves are gathered in large amounts for cooking as greens or for use like seaweed in sushi and tempura. The spikes of small fresh flowers are also delectable, and the seeds can flavor plum pickles and other sweet-and-sour foods.

In America, the red-leaved form of perilla was once favored as a garden plant, and can still be found in older gardens, keeping company with venerable peonies and antique roses. Along with old-fashioned balsam and spiderflower, this undemanding annual passed from one gardener to another, and the self-sowing plants found permanent homes in town and country gardens. Perilla today is enjoying a renaissance, both for

its decorative appeal and its tasty culinary possibilities. It also garnered attention recently due to the discovery that the oil from its seeds contains omega-3 essential fatty acids, famous for their potential to lower cholesterol. Once thought to be primarily a product of fish oils, omega-3's are now known to also be contained in some plant seeds, including flax and perilla.

The various forms of perilla include both plain or ruffled leaves of either red or green coloring. The red form provides bold, deep color among petunias, zinnias, and other annuals, where it can self-sow each year. Let it mix with bearded iris, perennial geraniums, and coreopsis: its strong color contrasts with almost anything. It also is pretty in shade gardens.

planting Easy from seed, sown directly in the garden in full sun to part shade, in well-drained soil.

cultivation Drought tolerant, shade tolerant. Pinch to keep plants bushy and compact, or let them grow to their full height of about 2 feet. Seed spikes, which look something like those of mints, add a touch of delicacy to the winter garden. All zones.

harvest Best used fresh. Cut back plant halfway to harvest large amounts of the foliage. Cut the flowers anytime for fresh use. Shake seeds into a paper bag when ripe.

Petroselinum crispum
parsley

Too bad so many sprigs of parsley go uneaten on restaurant plates—that little garnish of greenery packs a powerful punch of vitamin C, iron, and the natural antiseptic, chlorophyll. Besides its healthful effects, a nibble of parsley has a solid practical use for those dining out or in: it will erase any lingering hint of garlic or fish on the breath. Old-time herbalists believed that eating parsley warded off the intoxicating effects of overimbibing in wine, perhaps an attribute to swallow with the proverbial grain of salt.

In cooking, parsley is valued for its ability to notch up the flavors of other foods. It is a staple in Italian recipes, and adds a richer flavor to beef stew, poultry stuffing, and vegetable casseroles. Its own flavor is quickly lessened in cooking, however, so if you're making something less assertive than a tomato sauce, add parsley near the end of cooking to keep its distinctive savory-sweet taste. Chopped leaves liven up rice, grilled vegetables, and fish, and are delicious in mild cheese spreads. Try parsley butter, made with fresh, frozen, or dried leaves, on new potatoes, crusty bread, or corn on the cob.

Plain or curly is the question when it comes to parsley. Both are similar nutritionally, but flat-leafed "Italian" parsley is often more pungent, and the springy, tightly ruffled leaves of curly are used chiefly as a garnish. Grow within reach in pots, along walkways, as a ferny accent, or as a rich green edging to a bright flowerbed.

planting Seeds can take months to germinate. Sow a row in spring for next season's use, but buy young plants if you want a guaranteed crop within a matter of weeks. Grow in full sun to part shade, in rich, well-drained soil.

cultivation Parsley is biennial: it forms only leaves its first year, then flowers and dies the next. Plant anew each year for a continual supply. Black swallowtails may lay eggs on them; check for striped caterpillars before you munch! All zones.

harvest Pick leaves anytime. Use them fresh or freeze. You can also dry parsley, although it tends to lose a lot of its flavor. For large quantities, cut up to half the leaves from the plant just above soil level.

easy freezing

Keep a supply of fresh-tasting parsley on hand by freezing it in zip-top plastic bags. Loosely stuff each bag with whole leaves and lay flat until frozen. Crumble the bag in your hand to "chop" frozen parsley before use.

Pimpinella anisum
anise

Licorice flavor isn't only for the candy counter. Its warm sweetness is tasty in grown-up treats, too, including baked goods, fruit soups, Indian cuisine—and of course adult-only liqueurs and aperitifs. Before you fire up the still to make a batch of homegrown Pernod or anisette, however, try the delicious licorice flavor of this annual herb in something that the whole family can enjoy: a comforting cup of warm tea, or a batch of savory cookies.

Fragrant anise has the alleged ability to stimulate the tastebuds into wanting more, which is probably why you can't eat just one black jellybean. Although its use has been largely out of favor in modern America for many years, it has been enjoying a renaissance as ethnic recipes are revived and shared. For an unusual summer treat, crush some anise seeds with a rolling pin and mix them among ice-cold watermelon chunks.

planting Easy from seed. Sow in a sunny spot with well-drained soil.
cultivation Self-sows. Grow in its own bed, or allow seedlings to crop up serendipitously. Looks like a spindly Queen Anne's lace. All zones.
harvest Gather foliage anytime for use fresh, dried, or frozen. Shake seedheads into a paper bag; let seeds dry for a week before storing in jars.

Potentilla spp.
potentilla, cinquefoil

Anything that could halt a toothache was treasured in the days before preventive dentistry, and potentilla root quickly became a staple in the home herb supply. More than 400 species answer to the name *Potentilla*, and herbalists tended to concentrate on a few favorites that are close at hand. While Europeans were packing their painful teeth with the root of their local species, for example, natives of Mexico and the desert Southwest were chewing on a plant native to their area. Various potentillas were also used for dysentery, jaundice, gonorrhea—and for tanning leather, a tribute to the potency of the astringent root. The cheerful red leather trim of Laplanders' reindeer-fur outfits was dyed with the root. You're likely to meet a member of this tribe as a weed in your garden; or invite in any of the cultivated species for their abundant blossoms, which look like small wild roses.

planting Grow from purchased plants for bloom the same year. Plant in sun, in well-drained soil.
cultivation Highly adaptable and long-lived. Choose a permanent site; the taprooted plant is difficult to transplant. Zones 2–9.
harvest Do not use medicinally. Press flowers and interesting foliage of weedy or cultivated species for notecards and crafts.

Prunella vulgaris
self-heal

This useful plant often shows up in the rogues' gallery pictured on bottles of weed-killer, next to dandelions, violets, and other plants that dare to infiltrate precious lawngrass. Before you reach for the spray bottle, consider all the good this unassuming little creeper once did. Made into a tea, it banished worms and stopped internal bleeding. Sore throats or tonsillitis were soothed after a good gargle with it. Smashed and applied to fresh wounds, it halted bleeding and speeded up healing. It was even used to expel devils from the afflicted, putting an end to supernatural fits.

Give self-heal a small patch for its creeping stems to spread and root into a thick mat. In late spring, and sporadically through late fall, it is decorated with short upright spikes of deep blue-purple flowers that are beloved by bees and butterflies. The plants also make a good groundcover; mix them with English daisy and Roman chamomile for a small herbal lawn.

planting Easy to grow from plants transplanted from the lawn, or purchase young plants. Grow in full sun to light shade, in average soil.

cultivation Propagate by division at any time during the growing season; stems root quickly. Thrives in wet soils as well as those that are well drained. Zones 5–8.

harvest Collect fresh leaves in summer and brew into a tea for gargling or to soothe burns or cuts.

Pulmonária officinalis
lungwort

"Wort" shows up a lot in plant names, because it means exactly that: "a plant." In this case, the wort has leaves shaped like a human lung, round at one end, pointy at the other, and frequently spotted. Ancient herbalists practicing the Doctrine of Signatures, in which plants were selected according to the body part they resembled, took one look at this perennial herb and used it on those patients whose wheezing breath or hacking cough indicated that perhaps their lungs resembled lungwort's blotchy leaves.

Interestingly, they weren't far off-base, although their reasoning may have been a little sketchy. Lungwort is an effective expectorant, perhaps because its leaves contain silica, an irritant to the respiratory system.

If you want to experiment, stick to brewing a mild tea and using it very occasionally. But feast your eyes on lungwort all you like—it's a standout in the shady garden. You'll find a whole parade of lovely cultivars, with leaves stippled, marbled, spotted, and blotched with white and cream. The pink or blue flowers are reminiscent of Virginia bluebells, and just as fleeting, but the foliage remains glorious all season, lighting the garden with dappled silver. Combine the simple shape of lungwort leaves with plain-colored hostas or ferns. It spreads moderately in moist, humusy ground, forming a significant clump. The leaves dry nicely to add an unusual touch to potpourri or to pressed-plant crafts.

planting Buy young plants; lungwort rarely sets seed and all fancy cultivars are divisions of the parent plant. Grow in part to full shade, in moist but well-drained soil that is rich with humus.

cultivation Water regularly and mulch with chopped leaves to keep soil moist and loose. Propagate by division after flowering. Prone to drought-induced mildew; if leaves discolor, cut off affected leaves at ground level and allow to regrow. Zones 2–8.

harvest Collect leaves after flowering and dry them for tea or crafts.

Rhus glabra
smooth sumac

A few shrubs add permanent structure to an herb garden, and they also remind us that not all herbs are soft green plants. Many woody plants were used medicinally, as early civilizations experimented with the possibilities of plants. Sumac, a group of American shrubs, was used by native Americans in doctoring a number of common ailments. Smooth sumac was one of the most widely used, although staghorn and shining sumacs were also of value.

Brewed into a tea, the sour lemony berries reduced fever and soothed sore throats and mouth sores. Roots and branches were made into a decoction to treat gonorrhea, a trick that was quickly adopted by the Lewis and Clark expedition, who were likewise troubled with the affliction. Boiling the leaves and berries made a mash that relieved the infuriating itch of poison ivy and mosquito bites, which were a real plague on the outdoor societies of the time.

reduce smoking by sipping tea

One native American use of this small tree may show promise to modern civilization: smooth sumac was used to lessen the desire for smoking tobacco. Apparently the strong addictive quality of nicotine was a problem even then.

To try it yourself, steep 1 teaspoon of ripe smooth sumac berries in a cup of boiling water for about 20 minutes. Add a little honey to counteract the sourness of the fruit. Swallow a mouthful of the brew whenever you get the urge for a cigarette.

If the tea doesn't satisfy the cravings, you can also try smoking its dried leaves: they were used as a substitute when real tobacco was not available.

"officinalis": it's official

As you page through catalogs and references, you'll notice some plants include the word "officinalis" in their name (for example, *Pulmonaria officinalis*, *Salvia officinalis*). That's a clue that the plant was once held in high esteem by herbalists. Keep in mind, however, that the word is no guarantee of efficacy: it only indicates the plant was sold as an herb and widely accepted as an herbal treatment.

planting Buy young plants; they are tricky to identify in the wild and some (with white berries) are highly toxic. Plant in sun, in well-drained average soil.

cultivation Spreads by roots into a colony of small, suckering trees. Cut off shoots, or let it colonize a meadow or sunny bank, where its red fall foliage and berries will be assets. Cutting down the parent will induce a spate of progeny. Zones 2–8.

harvest Cut foliage anytime in season. Cut berries after a few frosts. Detach clusters to dry for teas.

Rosa spp.
roses

You would think that any plant that can cure the bite of a mad dog, regrow the hair on your balding head, and "make a face look young" would be tops in the garden—and thus it is with roses. Of course, the enduring popularity of roses has more to do with the beauty of the flowers than the unfounded claims of herbalists of yore. They are simply irresistible, with their lavish blooms, soft or saturated colors, and that unmistakable fragrance that thankfully is being restored to modern hybrids.

Roses look great nestled among perennials or annuals, where their height adds variety to the bed. Plant lavender, thymes, artemisias, salvias, and other low growers around their feet to blend bushes into the garden. Be sure to keep them within sniffing distance, though—a big part of the pleasure is inhaling their heavenly scent.

Rugosa roses and many old shrub roses, plus a plethora of modern hybrids, are nearly carefree. Unfortunately, that can't be said for dozens of others. As the rose craze swelled, less attention was given to survival than to making the biggest, boldest, best-looking flowers. Nowadays, though, you will find many of these flowers bred specifically for their hearty constitutions. Read the fine print on labels and in catalogs to find out if the rose you've fallen in love with is disease-resistant.

Planting a mixture of types will give you roses from spring through frost. In mild climates, they bloom right through winter. One of the delights of growing roses is that unexpected last flower of the season, which usually shows up long after the peak of the show, as days grow shorter in fall. The last rose of summer is more a thrill than all the abundance of June.

The fruit or "hips" have been treasured herbally for thousands of years. High in vitamin C, the hard red or orange berries were packed for long sea journeys, and later collected by volunteers to keep British soldiers healthy during World War II. Brew a cup of rosehip tea yourself as preventive medicine against winter colds and flu. The petals also pack a punch: their astringent properties tighten the skin and shrink pores. The edible petals add color strewn atop iced cakes or fruit salads.

rose follies and fancies

Beloved roses figure in myths and fairytales, the classics of Shakespeare, war, religion, and of course romance. If the price of a Valentine's Day dozen makes you shudder, consider Cleopatra: the sails of her ship were soaked in rose water so that perfume announced her arrival. The Roman emperor Heliogabalus literally smothered his guests, by filling the room with so many rose petals there wasn't much space to breathe. At the other extreme Saint Francis of Assisi supposedly turned his mind from temptation by rolling in a thicket of thorny rose canes whenever a lowly urge threatened his serenity.

planting Plant bareroot roses in early spring; plant potted roses anytime. Choose a spot in sun in rich, loose, well-drained soil.

cultivation Monitor for black spot, aphid infestations, and other problems; remove affected parts. Rake up fallen leaves to minimize pests and diseases. In very early spring, prune and thin roses, removing dead canes and cutting back dead branch tips to a healthy bud. Hardiness varies; most, Zones 5–9.

harvest Cut flowers for bouquets. Collect petals for culinary or craft use. Gather hips when they change color in late fall; dry on screens or in arrangements.

Rosmarinus officinalis
rosemary

With its stiff, skinny leaves and piney fragrance, rosemary could be mistaken for a downsized conifer. But what a mistake that would be. This aromatic shrub imparts delicious flavor to lots of our favorite dishes, from spaghetti sauce to grilled chicken, to oven-roasted potatoes. Long-lived in milder climates, rosemary becomes a permanent player in the garden, thriving for decades. Many cultivars are available, from low-growing prostrate forms that look beautiful spilling over a stone wall to 6-foot-tall, bushy types ideal for hedges. You can indulge in it wherever you live: It flourishes in containers and grows to good size in just a single season.

Very popular in cooking, rosemary infuses mild foods with its flavor, making magic with grilled fish, baked eggplant, and tender lamb. Both dried and fresh leaves are highly aromatic. Add it to casseroles, soups, and tomato sauces, toss in salad and pasta, lay leafy stems on baking chicken, fish, or meats, and use to flavor oils and vinegars. Use to scent cosmetics and bath oil. To shoo mosquitoes, rub a fresh sprig on bare skin.

Abundant spikes of small blue, white or pink flowers in summer and year-round deep green foliage make rosemary valuable in perennial beds as well as the herb garden. Plant taller cultivars to frame your doorway, or flank a bench with plants within arm's reach. For a summer pot, combine it with sulphur-yellow 'Moonbeam' coreopsis and a ruff of white petunias.

planting Seeds are slow to get started; buy young plants. Grow in light, very well-drained soil, full sun.

cultivation Susceptible to scale; snip off affected branches. If you see delicate webbing on the branches, spray upper- and undersides of foliage vigorously with water to dislodge spider mites. Do not allow soil of container plants to dry out. In cold areas, mulch plants with a deep, light layer of dead leaves for winter protection. Propagate by layering, or take cuttings of young branches in summer. All cultivars are hardy in Zones 8–10; a few will even survive to Zone 5.

harvest Snip foliage anytime for use fresh or dried.

Ruta graveolens
rue

The softly textured blue-green foliage of rue is too good to ignore, but handle this herb with care: many people find they are allergic to the foliage, which can cause a blistering rash. Even seedlings pack a wallop. To prevent mishaps, keep it in flowerbeds, where its lacy leaves, mounding form, and unusual color make a fine partner for other perennials.

It was popular for its metaphysical properties, among them warding off witches, devils, and evil spells, as well as enhancing "second sight," the ability to predict the future. More prosaically, it was used to heal tired eyes and headaches. Forget about employing this herb for healing: not only is the foliage too risky to handle, its bitter alkaloids can cause spasms and even death.

Rue may irritate the skin, but it is delicious to the eye. For a romantic summer garden, nestle its soft foliage around pale pink old-fashioned shrub roses—and add a collar of honey-scented sweet alyssum to keep the rue out of reach.

planting Sow seed in pots or buy young plants; always handle with gloves and long sleeves. Grow in full sun, in well-drained, lean to fertile soil.

cultivation Wearing protective clothing, prune back in early spring to encourage dense and compact growth; otherwise, the plant may become loose and sprawly. Drought tolerant; adds lushness to the stark forms of aloe, cacti, and New Zealand flax (*Phormium* spp.) in a dry garden. Zones 4–10.

harvest Ornamental use only. Do not touch with skin.

Salix alba
white willow

Pussywillows are a favored harbinger of spring, but these trees and shrubs once had many more uses. Their thin branches were woven into mats and baskets; the bark was collected in spring to ease fever, pain, infections, and upset stomach.

Willows grow across North America, usually beside streams where their roots can suck up the water they crave. Invite them into your yard with care: the roots will seek out reliable sources of water, including underground pipes.

planting Plant a young tree in sun to part shade, at least 100 feet away from any underground pipes. Or grow in a wooden half-barrel.

cultivation Willows grow very fast, which creates weak wood that is prone to breakage. Prune back hard in late winter to keep in bounds.

harvest Saw off branches and strip bark in spring; soak 1 tbsp of bark in cold water for several hours, then boil for 10 minutes. Swallow the bitter decoction one mouthful at a time until symptoms subside—or pop an aspirin instead.

the first aspirin

Nibble a branch of white willow, and you'll taste a familiar bitterness: salicin, the forerunner of today's ubiquitous aspirin, infuses the bark of this tree. For more than 2000 years, folks reached for willow bark instead of the aspirin bottle.

Salvia officinalis
culinary sage

If you only know sage as dusty leaves in a jar on the spice rack, get ready for a pleasant surprise. Fresh sage has an unusual but lovely camphor-bitter lemon scent, a big improvement over the musky smell of the dried leaves. Sample this strong-flavored herb in small doses at first. Chop some fresh leaves to strew across omelets or drop into canned or fresh tomato soup, or bruise a few leaves and simmer in a cream sauce to serve over pumpkin-stuffed ravioli. Enjoy sage in its traditional role in poultry stuffing, pork roasts, or homemade sausages, and experiment with the herb in lentil, rice, and nut dishes, in mushroom or barley soups, and with grilled, baked, or steamed onions, potatoes, squash, carrots, eggplant, and other veggies.

While we think of sage as an herb to simmer in sauces and stir into stuffing, the ancients slugged it down straight, as a steaming tea. Sweetened with a dab of honey, sage tea is a soothing drink that will reduce symptoms of a cold, as well as laryngitis and sore throat.

planting Easy from seed, or buy young plants. Grow in well-drained, average to fertile soil, in full sun.
cultivation Cut back young branches in late winter to keep vigorous and compact. Couple the gray foliage and rich blue flowers with bright, silky poppies, daylilies, or roses. Good in containers, too. Propagate by cuttings or layering. Zones 4–10.
harvest Pick leaves anytime for use fresh or dried.

Salvia spp.
sages, salvias

So many salvias, so little garden space—culinary sage has roughly 750 relatives in the large genus whose Latin name translates roughly to "salvation."

One of the most dramatic is pineapple sage (*S. elegans*), a shrub-size beauty that explodes in fall with bright red flowers at the tip of every branch. Its foliage smells sublime, so plant it where you can snitch a sniff in passing, and be sure to dry some for potpourri. Clary sage (*S. sclarea*) is an old-fashioned cottage garden plant, another big one that tops out at about 5 feet tall and 4 feet across. Its unusual flowers get added color from bracts that may be tinted pink, purple, or blue. Try its leaves instead of culinary sage in recipes.

Three ornamental salvias are standouts: the hybrid *Salvia* x *sylvestris*, with its neat mounded habit and abundant deep blue-purple blooms, which bless the garden from late spring through fall; fire-engine-red scarlet sage (*S. splendens*), planted as a bedding annual since the turn of the last century; and blue salvia, or mealy-cup sage (*S. farinacea*, especially 'Victoria'), grown as an annual.

red or blue for hummingbirds

The tubular, nectar-rich blossoms of salvias—especially the red variety—are highly appealing to hummingbirds, and the spikes of outward-facing flowers are perfectly arranged to fit their hovering habits. Blue flowers are usually most attractive to bees, but hummers also seek them out. In fall, many blue-flowered species native to the Americas come into bloom, succoring the tiny birds on their flight southward. In the garden, any salvia will satisfy their sweet tooth; if you don't yet have a crew of regulars, plant red salvias to catch their attention.

planting Grow from seed started early indoors for flowering the same year, or buy young plants. Grow in well-drained, average to fertile soil, usually in full sun.

cultivation Choose salvias according to where you intend to use them in the garden; heights, habits, and bloom times vary widely. Easy to propagate by cuttings. Hardiness depends on species; many are hardy in Zones 4–10.

harvest Nip off individual flowers soon after they open to dry for potpourri or crafts. Pick leaves of aromatic cultivars anytime for potpourri or cooking.

Sambucus spp.
elder

During the Middle Ages, folks spent a lot of time trying to keep away evil spirits, which apparently must have been raising quite a ruckus. Elder was one weapon in this battle: plant it by the door and no bogeyman could enter; neither would the house be struck by lightning, nor assailed by witches. Of course, figuring out the habits of evil spirits was no easy job: contrasting lore held that elder was actually the home of witches, who disguised themselves as branches.

Native Americans were more down-to-earth. They made a tea from its roots to induce labor, relieve headaches, and clear mucus from the lungs, and simmered the flowers to wash sore eyes. Country folk embraced elder for its berries, which make excellent wine and jelly as well as a decent cough syrup. Dipped in batter and fried, the wide, flat blossom clusters—picked clean of insects—make tasty fritters topped with a dusting of powdered sugar. Dried and used in cosmetics, the white flowers have a reputation for bleaching freckles and whitening the skin.

Children of old also used elder, whittling the hollow stems into whistles or pipes, a hobby that may have caused nasty side effects. The stems, roots, and leaves contain cyanide-like elements and have a strong laxative effect. Skip the medicinal uses, but do gather berries to make jelly and wine. Be sure to strain out all seeds, which contain toxins. And imbibe sparingly, as the fruit has a bowel-loosening effect.

planting Buy young plants. American or common elder (*S. canadensis*) has dark purple fruit; *S. racemosa*, red berries; *S. caerulea*, blue berries. Grow in well-drained soil, in sun to shade depending on species.

cultivation Elders grow fast and spread quickly by underground roots. Give them a patch of their own, with a fence they can lean their berry-laden branches upon. Hardiness varies depending on species; *S. canadensis* thrives in Zones 3–8.

harvest Clip blossoms soon after opening. Swish in water to rinse out insects. Pick berries when fully colored. Songbirds adore the fruit.

elder flower wrinkle cream

Lacy white elder flowers were prized for their skin-tightening effects. Why not test their alleged abilities yourself? Dry blossom heads, face down, on a clean net curtain. Crumble a generous handful into a bowl, and gradually mix in a few tablespoons of plain yogurt until a thick paste is formed. Slather onto wrinkle-prone skin areas. Wait 15 minutes, then splash off with cold water and pat dry.

Sanguisorba minor
burnet

Close your eyes and sniff—is that a cucumber you're smelling, or a sprig of burnet? This ferny, evergreen perennial herb is perfect for sparking up salads, especially in winter when real cukes are hard to come by in the garden. The delicate leaves of burnet must be used fresh, but you'll be able to gather them at any season, even if you have to brush away snow.

Burnet loses flavor with cooking, so add it to soups and sauces at the last minute. Blend finely chopped fresh leaves into cream cheese or butter to spread on crackers, fish, or hot corn on the cob. You can use a stem of dainty leaves as a swizzle stick in mild mint teas or in ice water.

The taproot of a related perennial herb, great burnet (*S. officinalis*), was once used to tan leather and was occasionally employed medicinally although its high tannin content can affect the kidneys and liver.

Both species often escape from gardens and can be found growing wild in fields and roadsides in some areas of the country.

planting Easy from seed, or buy a young plant. Grow in full sun to light shade, in well-drained, lean to fertile soil.

cultivation The plant becomes lanky after flowering. Cut back to ground level and it will quickly put out new growth. Self-sows; clip faded flowers before they go to seed to reduce progeny. Zones 4–10.

harvest Cut leaves anytime for fresh use, or to press.

Santolina chamaecyparissus
santolina

Santolina is great to practice topiary skills on. With regular shearing, it grows dense and full and is easy to train into formal or fanciful shapes. This perennial shrubby herb holds its leaves all year, which makes it a favorite for knot gardens, low hedges, and decorative borders.

Both deep green and silver-leaved santolinas are available. Their year-round color is equally valuable in the garden and dried arrangements. In midsummer, the plants are topped by a crowd of neat yellow button flowers, which can also be dried to add color to wreaths and bouquets.

Take advantage of the softening effect of this herb by planting it along pathways or patios. Grow it in containers or windowboxes, too; its delicacy complements large-leaved scented geraniums. You can also use the quiet color of silver-gray santolina to calm a flower garden of hot colors, or as a step between clashing hues, such as not-quite-complementary roses.

planting Sow the slow-growing seeds in pots, or buy young plants. Grow in full sun, in well-drained soil of poor to average fertility. Rich soil causes lax plants and poor foliage color.

cultivation Cut back hard in early spring to make it bushy. Repeat after flowering, removing the flower stems and branch tips. Propagate by cuttings or layering in spring, or divide large plants. Zones 6–8.

harvest Clip foliage in spring and summer, cutting whole stems. For drying, snip flowers with long stems soon after they open.

Saponaria officinalis
soapwort

A froth of pink flowers that completely cover the spreading plants is soapwort's greeting to the warm days of summer. In its homelands of Europe and Asia, it covers large expanses with sweeps of color, and in North America, where the herb has escaped from gardens, it blankets roadsides with a solid swathe of pale pink that continues sporadically through the first frosts.

Like many old favorite flowers, soapwort comes with a list of nicknames: bouncing Bet, old maids' pink, and dog cloves were some of its aliases. It was also called bruisewort, because of its reputation for healing skin problems. No monikers were assigned to this easy-care perennial for its other uses, as an expectorant, a gout treatment, and a last-ditch effort against the growth of tumors. The root of soapwort is where the medicinal properties are concentrated. A decoction made from one heaping tablespoon of dried root in a cup of water was swallowed one mouthful at a time for an all-purpose dosage for targeted ailments.

Soapwort is most famous for the sudsy wash water made from its roots and stems, which contain saponin. Farmers used it to clean sheep before shearing, while cloth-makers washed their homespuns in it. Don't expect a high lather, as the dirt-cutting power of this natural soap relies on chemical action more than bubbles.

Give it plenty of elbow room in the garden. Its leaves are covered with a grayish bloom, like grapeskins, so even when not in flower it makes attractive groundcover, especially interspersed with rocks. Shoulder it with Siberian iris and other upright perennials for contrasting form, or let it meander among the cosmos and beebalm of a cottage garden. The pink, sometimes white, flowers have a light, sweet scent.

planting Seed is slow to sprout and must be planted in fall. For faster results, take cuttings from the wild in summer, or buy young plants. Grow in sun, in well-drained soil. Fertile soil encourages invasive growth; lean or stony ground slows the spread.

cultivation Pull up the creeping roots when they overstep allotted boundaries. Propagate by division or cuttings. May self-sow. Zones 4–10.

harvest Collect stems anytime. Cut stems of flowers soon after opening for fresh bouquets. Dig roots in fall and dry for later use.

lather up: camping trip shampoo

Travel-size plastic bottles make homemade shampoo more of a fun experiment than a necessity on modern camping trips, but it's still nice to know that the means to clean your hair exists in the wild, just in case Y2K comes around later than we thought. Gather two generous fistfuls of soapwort stems, clip them at ground level, and chop them coarsely. Combine with about 2 cups of water in a pan or a bowl and stir them vigorously to release the saponin. Strain and use as shampoo or laundry soap.

Satureja hortensis
summer savory

Just as its name suggests, this annual herb makes foods taste better. Its peppery flavor has hints of thyme. Often overlooked as a possibility for the cook's garden, savory turns ordinary side dishes like peas, green beans, baked or boiled potatoes, squash, cabbage, and lentils into treats that will make friends and family lick their lips and ask for more. Use its lively flavor to wake up fish, beef, and chicken recipes, too. To add a spicy tang to fried chicken or other breaded foods, mince fresh savory or crumble dried leaves into the bread crumbs. Summer savory tea eases stomach cramps and diarrhea.

It also has a long-standing reputation as an aphrodisiac, perhaps because of the way its sprightly flavor awakens the senses.

planting Easy from seed sown in sunny, well-drained soil of average to rich fertility.

cultivation As foolproof to grow as zinnias, summer savory requires attention only when its seedlings are very young, to prevent them being overshadowed by competing weeds. All zones.

harvest Gather foliage anytime for use fresh or dried; flavor best before bloom. Clip often to delay bloom and keep vigorous; once it sets seed, growth slows.

Satureja montana
winter savory

This is a perennial relative of summer savory, with a stronger personality and a coarse, piney flavor that needs an assertive companion food. Use it with venison and other game, or in patés. You can also mince it into bread crumbs for preparing trout or other fish, or chicken.

Curiously, one medicinal effect of winter savory was supposedly just the opposite of its summer cousin: instead of enlivening the libido, it was believed to quell sexual desire.

The fine leaves of this nearly evergreen perennial make it ideal to weave into knot gardens or train as a low hedge. It likes frequent shearings, growing bushy and dense. Its rich,

deep color is held through all but the hardest winters, maintaining a garden's structure as well as providing fresh flavor year round.

planting Hard to grow from the fine, erratic seed, so best to buy young plants. Grow in full sun, in light, very well-drained soil of average to rich fertility.

cultivation Add gravel or sand and compost to lighten heavy clay soils, or grow in free-draining pots. Zones 6–10; may survive milder Zone 5 winters.

harvest Clip foliage anytime, even in winter. Use fresh or dried in cooking. For an unusual fresh wintertime bouquet, combine glossy sprigs with a bit of holly or dress up its vase with a red bow.

Sempervivum spp.
hens-and-chicks, houseleek

Hens-and-chicks are best known as ornamentals or houseplants, but they once held a secure foothold in herbal lore. These pretty succulent rosettes, available in an array of shapes, sizes, and tints, are almost as soothing as aloe when broken leaves are applied to burns or slight cuts. You can also use the juicy leaves to take pain out of insect bites, sunburn, and even irritation caused by herbs such as nettles or rue.

Hens-and-chicks are a collector's dream. A fun way to get started is to buy a packet of mixed seed. Seeing what comes up is like watching the birth of kittens—each one can be a different color and shape, but all are delightful.

These tough plants thrive in places no other plant can grow. They snuggle happily into the merest crack in paving or rock walls. For a little surprise, fill a pedestal birdbath with potting soil and add a few starts. In the herb garden, they add lively texture to fine-leaved creeping thyme.

planting Sow seed indoors in pots, or buy young plants. Grow in full sun, in poor to fertile well-drained soil.

cultivation Offsets are quickly produced around the base of the parent plant. Separate these rooted starts in spring, and replant to expand your plantation—or trade with friends. Hardiness varies depending on species; many thrive in Zones 4–10.

harvest Break off a leaf whenever necessary and apply fresh juice to injured skin.

success in a strawberry pot

Tall containers with pocket planting holes around their sides are called "strawberry pots," although it's very difficult to grow juicy berries in them. Due to the arrangement of the pockets, soil at the roots of plants dries out rapidly. Instead of struggling with strawberries, fill these pots with hens-and-chicks, which thrive even in drought conditions. Push the roots of each plant firmly into place in the pocket, and settle a few at the top of the container. They will quickly become established and begin producing "chick" offsets that hug the sides of the pot.

Serenoa repens
saw palmetto

This palm-like shrubby plant once covered thousands of acres in coastal Florida and Georgia, where it formed the understory beneath taller palms and pines. As development ran like wildfire throughout the states, the plants were bulldozed wholesale, so that today they colonize only a fragment of their original holdings. Their loss is unfortunate because of the saw palmetto's place in the fragile southern coastal ecosystem. Observers of more mercenary bent have also been lamenting the destruction of the plants, because in recent years their sprays of berries have become a hot property for nonprescription herbal preparations.

Traditional herbal use esteemed the dark purple or black berries as a source of healing teas, particularly effective on respiratory ailments like bronchitis and asthma. Congestion is also said to be alleviated by sipping a cup or two of saw palmetto berry tea each day. If you suspect serious health problems, get the advice of a medical doctor before trying herbal remedies that may not be as effective as traditional modern medicines.

Saw palmetto needs a subtropical climate in order to flourish, although you can try to cultivate it as a houseplant or summer patio plant if humidity levels are high. Daily sprays with a fine misting device, to replicate the summer showers in its native habitat, also encourage its growth. The plant has a unique growth habit, with the thick, almost trunk-like root remaining below the ground and only the tuft of bold leaves waving above the soil.

planting Buy a potted plant. Grow in part to full shade, in sandy, fast-draining soil.

cultivation Clip off dead leaves as needed with pruners. May be successful in a large container filled with lightweight soilless potting mix. Supply a little supplemental moisture by misting the foliage daily in dry spells. Zones 8–10; potted, all zones.

harvest Berries ripen in mid-fall through winter. Clip the bunches, strip off the berries, and spread on screens to dry.

health benefits

Saw palmetto tea is supposed to increase sexual powers, a claim which may have led to one of its more modern uses. Today's herbalists have turned to the plant as an aid for prostate problems, an advertisement now under closer scrutiny by science. Early investigation shows promising results, and over-the-counter users are snatching up the hoped-for cure. The burgeoning number of asthma sufferers, too, are sampling saw palmetto, which has a long-standing reputation for soothing breathing difficulties. Because over-the-counter herbal preparations are mostly unregulated by the Food and Drug Administration, experimentation with this alternative treatment is a personal decision.

Solidago odora
goldenrod

A territorial thug, goldenrod is notorious for swallowing up more than its share of the garden. Its fast-spreading roots crowd out anything in its path. Yet sweet goldenrod (*S. odora*) and others of its ilk were once valued cures for everything from bee stings to flatulence to kidney stones.

Include goldenrod in a meadow garden, or grow it with beebalm, fall asters, and other tenacious types. Roots are fairly easy to get rid of, and self-sown seedlings can be hoed off or hand-pulled. The sprays of golden flowers are unsurpassed for attracting beneficial insects and monarch butterflies on fall migration.

planting Seed is hard to find; start with young plants. Grow in full sun in well-drained, lean to average fertility soil. Rich soil encourages faster spread.
cultivation Pull unwanted roots. Zones 2–10.
harvest Cut flowers soon after opening for fresh or dried bouquets, or to mash into a lotion for insect stings. Collect fresh anise-scented leaves anytime to steep as a medicinal tea.

not the hayfever culprit
Goldenrod comes into full bloom just as hayfever sufferers are reaching their sneezing, itchy-eyed peak. The real culprit, however, is ragweed, which usually escapes notice because its flowers are drab green. It sneaks into empty lots, along roads, and hides in flowerbeds. Unlike goldenrod, its pollen is windborne, so it easily reaches unfortunate noses.

Stachys officinalis
betony

One of the most widely used medicinal herbs, betony was good for curing dozens of complaints, or at least so proclaimed old-time herbalists. Science is still working to prove or disprove the claims. It is known to contain tannins, which are bitter substances that act as astringents, drawing out moisture. Old herbals recommend it for bronchitis, sore throat, profuse sweating, vein problems, and worms, an affliction thankfully rare these days. A simple use for the juicy stems is to apply them to minor cuts or skin blemishes. An old name, lousewort, refers to the odd belief that it caused sheep to become infested with lice if they ate it.

A cousin of betony, the velvety gray lamb's-ears, is better known by gardeners than this green-leaved perennial. The spikes of reddish purple flowers attract bees and other nectar lovers, and may even bring hummingbirds. Betony is a tall herb, with spikes as tall as 3 feet. You may encounter it in shady wild places where it has leaped out of an old garden. Purple coneflower and goldenrod make good partners.

planting Easy from seed. Grow more ornamental named cultivars from young plants. Plant in full sun to shade, in well-drained soil of average fertility.
cultivation Some varieties tend to spread; uproot as required. Propagate by division. Zones 4–8.
harvest Collect leaves anytime for making tea. Press individual flowers for paper and other crafts.

Symphytum officinale
comfrey

Stout and coarse, comfrey is an emphatic plant that's impossible to overlook. Its handsome leaves can reach almost a foot in length, and the plant in bloom towers to 5 feet. Comfrey blooms are fascinating to watch unfurl from buds. The flowering stem emerges in a tight coil of pink-tinged buds, and slowly relaxes into a curved stem strung with dangling blue bells.

It has been implicated as a liver carcinogen, so avoid comfrey internally. But do savor the knowledge that this stout herb once alleviated stomach, menstrual, and gastrointestinal distress. Externally, it is safe to use and speeds healing of cuts and burns. Boil the leaves and fish them out to make a poultice for minor wounds, insect stings, and other skin problems.

Once you plant comfrey, it's there to stay, so choose a site with care before you invite this deep-rooted perennial in. Removing adult plants is tedious, because new growth sprouts from bits of broken roots. Add the slimy rhizomes that gave the plant the nickname "slippery root," and you have another reason to keep it undisturbed.

planting Sow seed or buy a young plant; one is all you need unless you're planning a comfrey hedge. Grow in sun, in well-drained soil of lean–average fertility.

cultivation Cut back hard if it topples, or support with sticks. Pull out self-sown seedlings. Zones 3–10.

harvest Collect fresh leaves anytime. Press individual flowers for crafts.

Tanacetum balsamita
costmary

Fans of micro breweries and home brewing should get to know this lesser known herb, which was once wildly popular. Formerly known as alecost, this sturdy perennial was prized by brewmasters, who added its spicy, slightly minty leaves and flowers to all their beer. Meanwhile, on church pews in colonial New England, costmary was known as Bible leaf, thanks to the custom of tucking a sprig among the pages of the Good Book, both to mark the place and to impart an occasional whiff of sharp fragrance to clear a drowsy head after a long sermon.

Aromatic costmary is just as delightful in a steaming bathtub after a long day at work. You can also slice slivers of fresh leaf among boiled potatoes or into soups, salads, and poultry stuffing for a savory tang. Use it sparingly until you decide how strong you prefer its bold flavor.

planting Seed is difficult; start with young plants. Grow in sun, in fertile, well-drained soil.

cultivation Costmary flowers look like they belong on a different plant: they are sprays of small, delicate white daisies held atop the 3-foot-plant. Clip off flowers after they're done blooming. Zones 5–9.

harvest Pick fresh leaves anytime. Cut flowers for fresh bouquets. Dry leaves and flowers for potpourri or sachets.

Tanacetum parthenium
feverfew

A dainty cousin to costmary, this perennial puts forth a flurry of small white daisies above its airy, bright green foliage. Its common name is a matter of some dispute; apparently the plant was used more to dispel headaches than to alleviate fevers. Research is ongoing as to the herbalists' claims that feverfew cures migraine headaches; studies have turned up interesting side effects, including improved sleep and less arthritis pain. Whether these are wishful thinking or due to ingesting feverfew remains to be seen. Treatment, in any case, is less than pleasant owing to the bitter taste of the leaves.

Feverfew is a generous self-sower, but its offspring are always welcome. Young plants are easy to transplant to other locations, and their long bloom period—from rose season in early summer to aster time in fall—makes them a garden treasure. The masses of tiny white flowers mingle easily with lavender, catmint, salvias, and other flowering herbs.

planting Easy from seed; plants sprout in as little as 5 days. Grow in full sun to part shade, in well-drained, average to fertile soil.

cultivation Self-sows, or propagate by division. Often short-lived, but self-sowing ensures a new batch of feverfew every year. Zones 4–10.

harvest Pick leaves or sprigs of foliage to dry for use in pest-repellent sachets.

second round of bloom

Feverfew blooms most abundantly in summer, then continues to push out new clusters of its small white daisies for sporadic bloom through frost. To get a second full burst of fresh flowers, cut back the plants by about one-third after blooming. They will quickly produce new branches, reinvigorating the plant, and form a host of new buds.

Tanacetum vulgare
tansy

Tansy is one of the most commonly grown herbs, probably because it's also one of the easiest to grow—and therein also lies the problem. A particularly enthusiastic self-sower and a fast spreader, tansy quickly forms stout clumps of roots so thick that you can barely get a shovel into the clump. Unfortunately, except for dried flowers, tansy is also one of the least useful herbs. Its pungent foliage was once used in embalming and to expel worms, two applications that the modern herb gardener generally has little use for. Made into sachets or laid in among your clothes, the foliage can make a decent insect repellent.

planting Easy from seed, or buy young plants for bloom the same year. Grow in sun to part shade, in well-drained soil.

cultivation Keep tansy in a meadow or cottage garden, where its pushy ways won't become a nuisance, or confine to a large container to keep in bounds. Clip off flowers before they set seed to minimize self-sowing. Zones 3–10.

harvest Clip flowers for drying soon after they open. Gather the foliage anytime to dry for use as an insect repellent.

Taraxacum officinale
dandelion

Ever wonder how all those yellow flowers ended up dotting your lawn? Thank the efficient seed dispersal system of the widely despised dandelion, which sends its myriad seeds airborne, each equipped with its own mini-parachute, all set to make a landing and plague lawn lovers everywhere. Dandelions are so widespread throughout the world that their actual origin is somewhat in doubt: most authorities settle on Eurasia, which encompasses quite a lot of ground. In America, they raised their proud yellow heads soon after the first European settlers set foot on these shores. The rest is history.

Although lawn care companies have been supported for decades by the anti-dandelion crowd, there is a multitude of reasons to appreciate instead of annihilate this plant. First of all, it's downright tasty. Young leaves have a refreshing, slightly bitter flavor that perks up salads and soups. Tight flower buds contribute the same flavor with a satisfying bite-size crunch, although older buds are undesirable because their petals tickle the throat. For a sunny touch on casseroles, salads, and soups, tear apart a blossom and scatter some yellow petals across the surface. If you want to try a new zing in your coffee or cocoa, chop the dried roots into 2-inch pieces, roast at 300°F for about 10 minutes, grind, and add about a quarter teaspoon when brewing a cup.

Dandelion gets its name from the French *dent de lion*, or lion's tooth, referring to the jagged leaves. Amaze your children by making dandelion magic: Slice the bottom part of a flower stem into strips, using your fingernail. Dunk in a glass of ice water and the strips will instantly curl into tight coils.

planting Sow a row in the vegetable garden to make harvesting easier than scouting around the lawn. Plant in sunny, well-drained soil; if you intend to harvest roots, dig in liberal amounts of compost so that soil is loose in texture.

cultivation Invest in an inexpensive dandelion digger tool to evict self-sown strays. Zones 3–10.

harvest Pick leaves when young for mildest flavor. Older leaves are good in soups. Pick flower buds when small to medium size and tightly packed. Dig roots in fall for drying.

spring tonic or winter delight

To herbalists, dandelions are a dream come true. The plant is used by countryfolk as a spring tonic for its actions in stimulating the liver and kidneys to remove toxins from the body. Exactly how this occurs is explained by an old name for the plant: "piss-a-bed." High in vitamin A, vitamin C, and potassium, the tangy leaves invigorate a tired body after a winter with no fresh greens. Tea made from the leaves has been used to cure constipation and upset stomachs; a stronger infusion from boiled roots allegedly helps gallstones. To remove troublesome warts or corns, rub the milky juice from leaves or stem onto the skin. If all else fails, try a nip of dandelion wine, a legendary beverage to make you forget what ails you.

Thymus spp.
thymes

Variety is a big part of the fun with thymes:
these tiny-leaved perennial herbs come in all
sorts of colors, textures, and personalities.
There's culinary thyme, for instance, which
grows into an upright, bushy mini-shrub infused
with that familiar scent. Wooly thyme, a love-at-
first-sight herb, crawls closely along the ground,
making a blanket of fuzzy foliage that begs to be
touched. Lemon thyme bears golden leaves and
a clear sharp citrus scent. Add variegated types
with white-edged foliage (see photos, far right);
those with flowers in pink, red, purple, or white
(see right); those that smell like nutmeg or
camphor or caraway—you can fill a whole
garden with thymes without ever getting bored.

Thyme is easy to use in cooking, too, because
its flavor marries well with just about anything. It
makes all kinds of meats, poultry, fish, game,
stews, and soups taste better. On the vegetarian
side, it peps up rice, lentils, beans, potatoes, and

quick chicken dinner

1 Cook enough rice or
pasta for four servings.

2 Meanwhile, cut two
chicken breasts into
small chunks. Heat 2–3
tbsp olive oil in a skillet,

add chicken, and sauté
until meat is opaque.

3 Drain a jar of roasted
red peppers and add to
pan, with 2 cloves garlic,
minced, and 2 tsp fresh

thyme, chopped. Stir
until chicken is tender,
about 10 to 15 minutes.

4 Add chicken medley
to rice or pasta. Garnish
with sprigs of thyme.

other starches, and adds zip to any vegetable—from artichokes to zucchini. Mash it into butter for bread or corn on the cob, simmer it with garlic and rosemary in marinara sauces, make flavorful vinegar—the list is endless.

Aromatic thyme is also delightful in the bath, in lotions, in potpourri and sachets. It improves digestion, soothes a cough, eases asthmatic breathing, helps headaches, encourages sleep, and relieves flatulence. You can tuck it into herbal wreaths and dried arrangements.

Create a sampler in a large container, fill windowboxes, snuggle creepers among cracks in paving, cover sunny slopes, make a thyme lawn, or combine with flowers. The fine texture makes a luscious underpinning for a rose garden—and will also release a delicious fragrance when stepped upon.

planting Thyme species are easy from seed sown in pots, where you won't have to spend time weeding among the tiny seedlings. For fancy varieties, buy young plants or beg a start from a friend. Plant in full sun, in well-drained soil of lean to rich fertility.

cultivation Drought tolerant. Propagate by cuttings or division. Protect marginally hardy types with a deep mulch of loose leaves. Start cuttings in summer for potted plants to winter on a windowsill. Zones 5–10.

harvest Snip foliage anytime for fresh use or drying. To harvest large quantities, cut back plants by halfway in early summer; they'll quickly regrow.

Tropaeolum majus
nasturtium

Nasturtium flowers look like delicate exotics, but at heart they're downhome, kin to the wild yellow mustards that blanket spring fields and the lowly shepherd's purse that finds a home at roadside. All are members of the giant mustard family. Nibble a leaf—or a flower if you can spare one— and note the familiar peppery bite of a mustard. Use its leaves in salads, its spicy flowers to dress up open-face sandwiches or add a confetti touch to salads and rice, and try the crunchy buds fresh or pickled like capers.

Gratifyingly easy to grow, nasturtiums have seeds the size of green peas, ideal for a child to handle. They sprout seemingly overnight, and bloom in just a matter of weeks. Grow trailing types in windowboxes indoors or out, and use the bright red, orange, or yellow flowers to edge beds or add a dab of color in pots. The blossoms are adored by hummingbirds.

planting Easy from seed. Soak overnight in water for faster germination. Plant in full sun, in well-drained average to fertile soil.

cultivation Although usually grown as an annual, nasturtium is perennial in very mild climates. Cabbage butterfly caterpillars may eat the leaves; plant more in another location and enjoy the butterflies that hatch. Aphids are sometimes troublesome. All zones.

harvest Pick leaves or flowers anytime for fresh use. Grow indoors for winter salads.

Urtica dioica
stinging nettle

Take that name seriously. An up-close-and-personal encounter with this plant will leave your skin itching and burning for hours or even days. Stinging nettle has one of the most devilish arsenals in the plant kingdom. Beneath its leaves and covering its stems are zillions of tiny, hollow hairs that work like hair-trigger hypodermic needles. They actually inject their "venom" into the skin of anyone unlucky enough to blunder into the plant—or even lightly brush against it.

All the same, stinging nettle has been popular for centuries—as food, medicine, and for making cloth. One of the more bizarre uses to which the plant was put was described by the Roman, Petronius, who suggested that a cure for a lack of virility was to thrash the poor fellow with nettles in the, uh, nether regions. Less dramatic uses were achieved through nettle tea, said to relieve asthma and other breathing difficulties, diarrhea, and urinary problems. Hopeful folks rubbed nettle-root brew on heads to stimulate new hair. Practice positive thinking and try a homemade hair rinse; it may not grow a fresh crop, but will give remaining locks a lovely shine.

In spring, these wild greens make nutritious cooked vegetables when picked young. (If the leaves are mature, the stinging hairs can cause internal irritation.) They are rich in vitamin C, and mild in flavor. Prepare as you would spinach—but be sure to wear gloves and long sleeves when working with the greens.

Keep nettles in an out-of-the-way part of the garden, and think twice about growing them if you have small children. Red admiral butterflies seek out nettles to lay their eggs on; look for the spiny caterpillars or evidence of nibbled leaves.

planting Grow from seed started in pots, where you can keep an eye on them and avoid accidental contact. Plant in sun to shade, in fertile, moist soil.

cultivation Wear protective clothing whenever you approach the patch. No care is needed; nettles will flourish just fine when left to their own devices. Zones 3–10.

harvest Gather young shoots as soon as they appear in spring, and pick young leaves for cooked greens. Snip mature leaves anytime for hair rinses. Always handle with extreme caution.

Valeriana officinalis
valerian

You are getting sleeeepy, very sleeeepy. If you had just sipped a cup of valerian tea, it would be no surprise to find your eyelids growing heavy: the perennial herb has been used as a tranquilizer for centuries. Scientists still aren't sure just how valerian slows a body down, but they do know that ingesting too much can lead to dizziness, depression, and eventually stupor.

Cats will find this herb equally intoxicating, although they get that languorous feeling from scent alone. They adopt a planting as quickly as catnip, rolling in the foliage. Human noses have a hard time understanding the lure, because valerian can smell like stale sweat or old leather.

Growing to as much as 5 feet, valerian spreads into large clumps by underground roots and may also self-sow. Although it isn't as widespread a weed as other herbs such as chicory and Queen Anne's lace, valerian is often found growing wild in the Northeast around old homesteads, as a stray in meadows, or along streams.

Valerian is also called garden heliotrope, because at their best, the early summer flowers have a sublime scent. The fragrance can vary widely from one plant to another, so if possible, take a test sniff of the flowers before you buy. Dry the flowers for potpourri if you like the smell. Plant it in the back of the garden, where its clusters of tiny white or pinkish red flowers will provide a soft backdrop behind bearded iris, phlox, and other summer-blooming perennials.

planting Seed is difficult to start; buy young plants or ask a friend for a division. Grow in moist, fertile soil, in sun to part shade. Excellent near water.

cultivation Uproot runners to keep plants in bounds. Propagate by division. Zones 4–8.

harvest Avoid using the root medicinally, due to risk of overdose. Cut flowers soon after they open for fresh or dried bouquets.

Verbascum thapsus
mullein

"Velvet plant" is another name for this biennial herb, which puts forth a rosette of big, irresistibly soft leaves its first year, then erects a wooly poker of yellow flowers in its second summer. You'll see the remains of mulleins along many roadsides across America, where the once-treasured herb has gone wild. The tall, dark brown candelabra persist until spring, when they finally topple to make room for newcomers.

Mullein is a dramatic foliage plant for the herb or ornamental garden. The clump of soft, silvery leaves can spread to 2 feet across, making it as useful in the sunny garden as hosta is in the shade. The quiet color works wonders with hot magenta petunias, but also looks great with white flowers and silvery artemisias. Leave the stalk in winter to add height to the garden, and attract woodpeckers, searching out insects.

Brewed into a tea, the leaves stop wracking coughs and soothe irritated throats. The tea also calms digestive difficulties. To bring on sleep or

quiet aches and pains, the flowers too can be gathered for tea, using 1 teaspoon for each cup of hot water. If you're suffering from congestion, make a tent and breathe in the head-clearing vapors. Mullein flowers were also said to remove warts, and a poultice of boiled leaves may help heal cuts and abrasions.

worth a try as wart remover

Mullein's yellow flowers were just as valued by herbalists as the big gray-flannel leaves. To try them yourself as a homemade wart remover, crush a handful of fresh blossoms with the back of a spoon in a bowl. Pat onto the affected skin and wait about 15 minutes. Remove the flowers and allow the skin to dry. Reapply daily until warts hopefully disappear.

planting Scatter seed here and there in the garden in fall or spring. Grow in full sun, in well-drained, lean to fertile soil.

cultivation Its deep taproot makes mullein difficult to transplant, so work around volunteer seedlings instead of trying to move them. Zones 3–10.

harvest Slice off leaves at their base with scissors for fresh or dried use. Collect the flowers soon after opening.

Verbena officinalis
vervain

Vervain's romantic story begins with the goddess Isis, shedding tears for her dead lover. Wherever a tear fell, so the story goes, vervain would then spring up.

Treasured since ancient times for its healing properties, vervain was believed to stop spasms, quiet raging fevers, and heal kidney and liver afflictions. Applied externally, it was used for skin rashes and cuts. It was also sampled by men as a marital aid in pre-Viagra days.

Vervain tends to look more weedy than ornamental, but its skinny, branching spires of tiny whitish flowers have an airy look that is pretty with bright red flowering geraniums or scented geraniums of interesting texture planted in front of it.

planting Easy from seed. Grow in full sun to part shade, in moist but well-drained fertile soil.
cultivation Pull out self-sown seedlings when young. Mulch to retain moisture. Zones 5–8.
harvest Collect leaves before flowering occurs in summer to fall. Chop 1 tbsp and soak in cold water overnight to make a treatment for skin irritations. Avoid taking internally; nausea and vomiting can occur even with moderate doses.

Vinca major, V. minor
periwinkle

Well known as a reliable, free-blooming ornamental groundcover, periwinkle has a distinctive lavender-blue color that is lovely with daffodils, tulips, and other spring bulbs. Two species are commonly grown: *V. minor*, a popular evergreen groundcover; and *V. major*, a taller and more tender type. Both bloom early in spring and continue putting forth a few new flowers through much of the year.

Traditional uses included treating diarrhea and hemorrhage: periwinkle's astringent properties apparently aid in stopping the free flow of various body fluids. Enjoy it for its beauty instead of its curative value: just gazing upon the sea of "periwinkle blue" works wonders to calm you down. Both make dense, evergreen groundcovers, beautiful with ferns or hostas for textural accent, or as a cloak for spring bulbs.

planting Buy multipacks of young plants in spring. Grow in sun to shade, in moist to well-drained soil.
cultivation Highly adaptable, growing well in a variety of soils and conditions. They spread fast through underground roots and may become invasive. Plant as groundcovers. Propagate by division or cuttings. *V. minor*, zones 4–10; *V. major*, zones 7–10.
harvest Do not use medicinally. Press the flowers for notecards and other crafts.

Viola spp.
violets, pansies

Old-fashioned charm is what you'll get when you plant violets. These carefree perennials are so easy to grow that they show up on the labels of some weedkillers as an undesirable. Don't let that deter you: if perfect lawngrass is important, you can easily lift strays and pop them back into the garden. Dozens of species of violets spread across the world, but by far the most commonly found species in America is the sweet violet (*V. odorata*), a hardy species with color that lives up to its name. The world of violets is fascinating once you begin exploring: check specialty plant catalogs for blue-and-gray Confederate violets, burgundy-leaved Labrador violets, long-spurred dog violets, bright blue birdsfoot violets, downy yellow wood violets, and dainty white violets.

One step away from violets are violas, which look more like small pansies than a nosegay of violets. Less cold hardy, they're often planted in masses or in containers as early spring annuals. Pansies are ever popular, with romantic new colors and ruffled shapes showing up every year at garden centers. Recently, they've been bred for more cold tolerance, with some strains able to survive through a Zone 6 winter.

Once used medicinally, violets are today known best for their edible flowers. Dip small blossoms in sugar syrup for candied ornaments to top desserts, or use flowers to add color to green salads, melon, or fruit. Freeze smaller flowers in ice cubes to add pizzazz to ice water.

planting Some violet species can be grown from seed, but many are sold as young plants. Buy them in multipacks, or start seed indoors in winter for spring bloom. In general, they prefer a shady or partly shady site with loose, humusy soil and plenty of moisture, but required conditions vary according to species. Pansies and violas thrive in containers.

cultivation Uproot stray plants as desired, or let violets spread as a quaint groundcover. Fritillary butterflies seek the plants to host their young.

harvest Pick blossoms soon after opening, for pressing or eating.

index

a

aches and pain soother 88
Achillea millefolium See yarrow
aching joints 67
acid soil herbs 26, 27
acne treatment 143
   See also skin remedies
Aconitum spp. *See* monkshood
Acorus calamus See sweet flag
afterbath oil 153
Agastache spp. *See* anise hyssop
Agrimonia eupatoria See agrimony
agrimony 78
air fresheners 69
Alchemilla mollis See lady's mantle
alkaline soil herbs 26
allergy relief 112
Allium spp. 82
   A. giganteum 82
   A. moly 82
   A. sativum See garlic
   A. schoenoprasum See chives
aloe 83
   for medicinal use 20
   for patios 21
   for skin problems 67
Aloe vera See aloe
Aloysia triphylla See lemon verbena
Althaea officinalis See marsh mallow

b

bad breath 67
balconies, herbs for 21–22

Anethum graveolens See dill
angelica 86
   harvesting 59
   positioning 14
   shape 13
   soil conditions 27
Angelica archangelia See angelica
anise 156
   collecting 58
   harvesting 59
   medicinal use 67
   uses 60
anise hyssop 78
Anthriscus cerefolium See chervil
antibacterials 67
aphids 49
Arctium lappa See burdock
Armoracia rusticana See horseradish
artemisia 89
   knot gardens 17
Artemesia spp. *See* artemisia
   A. dracunculus 'Sativa' See tarragon, French
   A. tridentata See sage, sacred
arthritis 68
artichoke for impotence 66
Asian cuisine herbs 19, 109

basil 146–7
   collecting 58
   companion plants for 37
   culinary use 62, 65
   diseases 49
   for indoor growing 10
   parterres 19
   for pests 49
   planting 34
   'Purple Raffles' for decoration 69
bath
   oils 73
   relaxation 77
bay 131
beans, herbs for 63
beebalm 143
   collecting 58
   for cosmetics 72, 73
   for decoration 69
   diseases 49
   to encourage wildlife 74
   for groundcover 23, 44
   medicinal use 67
   soil conditions 27
   tea 63
beef, herbs for 63
Bellis perennis See daisy, English
betony 174
biscuits, herbs for 63
blazing star, uses 60
boneset 117
borage 92
   collecting 58
   companion plants for 37
   decorative flowers 92
   planting 34
Borago officinalis See borage

border herbs 14–15
broken heart, herbs for 67
bulb herbs 32, 34
burdock 87
   harvesting 59
   planting 34
   uses 60
burnet 167
butter, herbs for 63
butterflies, encouraging 74

c

cakes, herbs for 63
Calendula officinalis See marigold, pot
caliche soil herbs 26
cancer treatment 68, 99
candles 71
Capsella bursa-pastoris. See shepherd's purse
Capsicum frutescens See cayenne pepper
caraway 97
   collecting 58
   harvesting 59
   medicinal use 67
   pests 49
   positioning 14
cardamom 114
   saffron rice with 106
   uses 60
carrot, wild 110
   dried 110
   to encourage wildlife 74
   uses 60
Carthamus tinctorius See safflower

Carum carvi See caraway
Cassia marilandica See senna
caterpillars 48
Catharanthus roseus See periwinkle, Madagascar
catnip 145
   companion plants for 37
cayenne pepper 94–95
   for patios 21
   safety 95
Centranthus rubber See valerian, red
Chamaemelum nobile See chamomile
chamomile 100–1
   for cosmetic use 20, 72, 73
   for groundcover 44
   for hyperactivity 66
   for medicinal use 20, 67
   in paths 23
   planting 34
   positioning 15
   tea 63
   wheel gardens 18
chamomile, German 138
   for hanging baskets 13
   for indoor growing 11
   for lawns 22
   tea 138
cheese hors d'oeuvres 119
chervil 86
   medicinal use 67
chicken
   dinner recipe 180
   herbs for 63
chicory 13, 34, 102
   harvesting 59

chives 81
  collecting 57
  companion plant for 37
  culinary use 62, 65
  division 51
  kitchen gardens 14
choosing your herbs 9, 30
cicely See sweet cicely
Cichorium intybus See
    chicory
cilantro See coriander
cinquefoil See Potentilla
    spp.
citrus scented herbs 20
clay soil 27
climate needs of herbs 24
cloches 47
clothes freshener 73
Cnicus benedictus See
    thistle, blessed
coffee
  chicory 102
  dandelion 179
  herbs for 63
cold frames 47
comfrey 175
companion planting 37
compost
  for fertilizing 45
  for herb planting 27, 29
compress 68
coneflower, purple 112
  to encourage wildlife 74
constipation 67
container herbs 11–13, 21,
    27, 171
  planting up 36, 171
  weeding 44
cookies, herbs for 63
coriander 105
  collecting 58
  companions plant for 37
  disease 49
  for impotence 66
  kitchen gardens 14
  medicinal use 67
Coriandrum sativum See
    coriander
cosmetic uses for herbs
    20

cosmetics 72–73
  dangerous 110
costmary 176
cottage garden herbs 16
crab, herbs for 63
cream cheese, herbs for
    63
Crocus sativus See
    saffron
cucumber 107
  planting 34
  trailing, for patios 21
  uses 60
Cucurbita pepo See
    cucumber
culinary herbs 62–64
  for patios 21
  theme gardens 19
cuttings 53
Cymbopogon citratus See
    lemongrass

d

daisy, English 91
  lawns 22
dandelion 179
  medicinal use 67, 179
  planting 34
dangers of herbs 115, 127
Daucus carota See
    carrot, wild
decking, herbs for 21–22
decoction 68
decorative herbs for home
    69–71
deodorizer for hands 141
depression 127
desert tea 68, 114–15
digging tools 40
digitalis for heart
    conditions 66
Digitalis purpurea See
    foxglove
dill 85
  attracting insects 38
  collecting 57, 58
  companion plant for 37
  to encourage wildlife 74

harvesting 59
  kitchen gardens 14
  medicinal use 67
  planting 34
  positioning 14
diseases 48–49
division 51–52
Doctrine of Signatures 124
drainage needs for herbs
    27
dry soil herbs 26, 27
drying herbs 59–60, 110
  for decoration 69
dyeing 96, 106

e

Echinacea spp. See
    coneflower, purple
eczema 68
edible flowers 65
  garnishes 64–65
eggs, scrambled, herbs for
    63
elder 166–7
elderberry uses 60
elecampane 129
Elettaria cardamomum
    See cardamom
Ephedra spp. See desert
    tea
Eupatorium spp. See hemp
    agrimony
  E. maculatum/
    purpureum See Joe
    Pye weed
  E. perfoliatum See
    boneset
  E. rugosum See
    snakeroot, white
Euphorbia robbiae See
    spurge
evening primrose 148
  uses 60, 67, 123

f

facial cooler 107
fennel 119
  attracting insects 38

color 14
  culinary use 65
  medicinal use 67
  planting 34
fertilizing 45
  container growing 12
feverfew 176–7
fish, herbs for 63
flatulence 67
flax 136–7
flea beetle 49
flowers, edible 65
Foeniculum vulgare See
    fennel
foot balm 78
formal garden herbs 17–19
foxglove 110–11
  planting 34
Fragaria vesca/virginiana
    See strawberry, wild
freezing herbs 60, 61, 92,
    155
fruit, herbs for 63
fusarium wilt 49

g

Galium odoratum See
    sweet woodruff
garden heliotrope See
    valerian
garden herbs 13–23
garlic 80–81
  collecting 58
  companion plant for 37
  culinary use 62
  harvesting 59
  planting 34, 35
  preserving 80–81
garnishes 64–5
geranium, scented 153
  apple 13
  for cosmetics 73
  for indoor growing 10
  soil for pots 12
  for themed garden 20
German cuisine herbs 19
gill-over-the-ground See
    ground ivy

ginger medicinal use 67
Gingko biloba for memory
    loss 67
ginseng 150
glass cover for herbs 47
Glechoma hederacea See
    ground ivy
goldenrod 174
  to encourage wildlife 74
  medicinal use 67
  positioning 15
gravel for herbs 29
  mulches 45
ground ivy 122–3
groundcover herbs 22–3

h

hair rinse 101
Hamamelis virginiana See
    witch hazel
hanging baskets for
    container herbs 13
hangover 67, 68
hardiness zones 24
hardpan soil herbs 26
harvesting 56-59
hayfever 174
heartburn soother 110
heartsease, medicinal use
    67
hedges, herbs as 23
hemp agrimony 117
hens-and-chicks 171
  for hanging baskets 13
  medicinal use 67
  for patios 21
  for walls 23
Hepatica nobilis 124
Hibiscus spp. 124–5
  hedges 23
  for indoor growing 11
  soil conditions 27
hiccups 67
horseradish 88
  collecting and
    harvesting 58, 59
  for medicinal use 20, 67
  pests 49

planting 34, 35
sauce 88
hoses 40
houseleek See hens-and-chicks
hummingbirds, encouraging 74, 143
hummus, herbs for 63
Hypericum spp. *See* St. John's wort 127
hyssop 128
planting 34
See also anise hyssop
Hyssopus officinalis See hyssop

i

iced tea 64
immune system boosting 112
indigestion 67
indoor herbs 10–11, 46
informal garden herbs 14–16
infusion 68
insect stings 67
insects
attracting beneficial 38
removing 64
repelling 94, 168
insomnia 67
Inula helenium See elecampane
Ipomoea spp. *See* morning glory
I. pandurata See man-of-the-earth
Italian cuisine herbs 19
itch soother 87

j

Japanese beetle 49
Joe Pye weed 116
positioning 14
shape 13
uses 60

Jupiter's beard 100
planting 34

k, l

kitchen gardens 14
knot garden herbs 17
lady's mantle 79, 111
lamb's-ears 174
Laurus nobilis See bay
Lavandula spp. *See* lavender
lavender 132–3
for cosmetic use 20, 72, 73
disease 49
to encourage wildlife 74
for indoor growing 10
lotion 72
medicinal use 67
planting 34
for special places 21
soil for pots 12
lawn herbs 22–23
layering 54
leaf spot 49
leaves, collecting 57–58
lemon balm 139
for cosmetics 72
disease 49
medicinal use 67
pests 49
planting 34
lemon butter cookies 84
lemon verbena 84
for cosmetics 73
for indoor growing 11
pests 49
lemongrass 108–9
for indoor growing 11
storage 109
tea 63
winter protection 46
Leonurus cardiaca See motherwort
lettuce, companion plant for 37
Liatris spicata See blazing star 135

licorice scented herbs 20
light conditions for herbs 26
linen freshener 73, 109
Linum spp. *See* flax
lotions 72
lovage, medicinal use 67
lungwort 158

m

Madagascar periwinkle 99
maintenance of herbs 41–49
mallows 124–5
man-of-the-earth 130
marigold, pot (calendula) 93
for cosmetics 72
for decoration 69
disease 49
medicinal use 67
uses 60
marjoram 148
medicinal use 67
marsh mallow 124
Matricaria recutita See chamomile, German
medicinal herbs 20, 66–68
Melissa officinalis See lemon balm
Mentha x *piperita See* peppermint
M. pulegium See pennyroyal
M. spicata See spearmint
Mexican cookery 19, 105
microwaving herbs 60
Middle Eastern cuisine herbs 19
mildew 49
mint
collecting 57, 58
companion plant for 37
culinary use 65
disease 49
for groundcover 23
medicinal use 67

pests 49
positioning 15
spreading problem 43
for themed garden 20
mint julep 140
misting attachment for hose 40
Monarda spp. *See* beebalm
monkshood 77
morning glory 130
planting 34
moth repellent 168
motherwort 134-5
mouthwash 98
mulching 43, 44–45
mullein 13, 185
multiple sclerosis 68
Myrrhis odorata See sweet cicely

n

nasal congestion 67
nasturtium 182
companion plant for 37
disease 49
to encourage wildlife 74
pests 49
Nasturtium officinale See watercress
Nepeta cataria See catnip
nerves, frazzled 67
nettle, stinging 183
niche herbs 23
notecards 71

o

obesity 68
Ocimum spp. *See* basil
Oenothera biennis See evening primrose
oils
herb 60–61
scented 71
oregano
collecting 58
culinary use 62, 65
disease 49

to encourage wildlife 74
groundcover 44
medicinal use 67
pests 49
soil for pots 12
uses 60
organic control of pests and diseases 48
organic mulches 45
origanum 149
Origanum majorana See marjoram
O. vulgare See origanum
orrisroot 71
Oswego tea 143

p

Panax quinquefolius See ginseng
pancakes, herbs for 63
pansy 187
Papaver spp. *See* poppy
paper 71
parsley 155
collecting 58
culinary use 62
to encourage wildlife 74
freezing 155
kitchen gardens 14
medicinal use 67
planting 34
parterre herbs 18–19
paths, herbs in 23, 101
patio herbs 21, 125
Pelargonium spp. *See* geranium, scented
pennyroyal 141
peppermint 140
for medicinal use 20, 67
tea 63, 140
peppers, culinary use 62
Perilla frutescens 154
color 14
for decoration 69
periwinkle 186
periwinkle, Madagascar 99
medicinal use 67

pesto 147
pests 48–49
  repellents 94, 168
Petroselinum crispum See
  parsley
pillow sweetener 121
Pimpinella anisum See
  anise
planting herbs 32–38, 44
poppy 150
  planting 34
potato salad, herbs for 63
potatoes, herbs for 63
Potentilla spp. 156
potpourri 70–71
pots for container herbs
  11–12, 21, 22
poultice 68
poultry, herbs for 63
premenstrual syndrome 68
pressed herbs 110
propagation 50–55
Prunella vulgaris See self-
  heal
pruning 13, 23
Pulmonaria officinalis See
  lungwort

q, r

Queen Anne's lace 86, 110
ragweed 174
raised bed herbs 15–16
recipes, cosmetic/
    medical/household
  aches and pains 88
  acne treatment 143
  afterbath oil 153
  allergy relief 112
  deodorizer for hands
    141
  eye soother 123
  facial cooler 107
  foot balm 78
  hair rinse 101
  heartburn soother 110
  linen/pillow sweetener
    109, 121
  moth repellent 168

mouthwash 98
pest repellent 94, 109
relaxing bath 77
scented stationery 132
shampoo 72, 169
skin remedies 72, 76, 83,
    82, 143
sting soother 87
warts 179
wrinkle cream 157
yellow dye 96
recipes, culinary
  cheese hors d'oeuvres
    119
  chicken dinner recipe
    180
  chicory coffee 102
  dandelion coffee 179
  herb vinegar 61
  herbal teas 64, 138, 139,
    140, 143, 159, 160
  horseradish sauce 88
  lemon butter cookies 84
  Mexican cookery 105
  mint julep 140
  pesto 147
  saffron rice with
    cardamom pods 106
  savory herb oil 61
Rhus glabra See sumac,
  smooth
rice, herbs for 63, 106
rock garden herbs 16
rolls, herbs for 63
roof gardens, herbs for
    21–22
root herbs 34
roots, digging up 59
Rosa spp. 160–1
  for decoration 69
rose chafer 49
rose mallow 124
rosehip tea 63, 160
Rosmarinus officinalis See
  rosemary
rosemary 162
  collecting 58
  companion plant for 37
  for cosmetics 72
  culinary use 62

pests 49
  types 13
  for walls 23
rotation 48
rue 163
  companion plant for 37
Ruta graveolens See rue

S

safety of herbs 115, 127
safflower 96
  for decoration 69
saffron 106
  planting 34
  rice with cardamom
    pods 106
sage 165
  clary 165
  culinary 164
  collecting 58
  companions plant for 37
  to encourage wildlife 74
  knot gardens 17
  medicinal use 67
  positioning 14–15
  pineapple 165
  sacred 90
sagebrush 90
salads, herbs for 63
Salix alba See willow,
  white
Salvia spp. *See* sage
  S. elegans See sage,
    pineapple
  S. farinacea See sage
  S. officinalis See sage,
    culinary
  S. sclarea See sage,
    clary
  S. splendens See sage
  S. x superba See sage
Sambucus spp. *See* elder
sandwiches, herbs for 63
Sanguisorba minor See
  burnet
Santolina
    chamaecyparissus
    168

Saponaria officinalis See
  soapwort
Satureja hortensis See
  savory, summer
  S. montana See savory,
    winter
savory
  summer 170
  winter 170
saw palmetto 173
  medical uses 67, 173
scale insect 49
scented herbs 72–73
  for patios 21
  for potpourri 70–71
  for stationery 132
  theme garden 19, 20
seafood, herbs for 63
seed herbs 32–34
  collection 50, 58–59
  equipment for starting
    39
  propagation 50–51
  self-seeding herbs 16
  storage 51
seedlings, weeding 42
self-heal 157
  for lawns 22
Sempervivum spp. *See*
  hens-and-chicks
senna 98
Serenoa repens See saw
  palmetto
shade, herbs for 25
shampoos 72, 169
shepherd's purse 94
shovels 40
sinus congestion 67
site preparation for herbs
    28–29
skin healing remedy 72,
    76, 83, 92, 143
sleeplessness remedy 138
smoking, stopping, help
  for 159
snakeroot, white 117
soaps 72
soapwort 169
  for cosmetics 72
  soil

conditions for herbs
    26–27
  for container growing
    12, 22
  preparation for herbs
    28-29
Solidago odora See
  goldenrod
sore throat remedy 135
soups, herbs for 63
spearmint 142
spider mite 49
spurge 118
St. John's wort 126–7
  for depression 67
Stachys officinalis See
  betony
stems, collecting 57–58
stews, herbs for 63
sting soother 67, 87
stinging nettle 183
stomachache 67
storage 59–60
strawberry, wild 120
sucker separation 51
sumac, shining,
    propagation 51
sumac, smooth 159
summer savory
  companion plant for 37
  culinary use 62
  medicinal use 67
swallowtail butterfly larva
    48
sweet cicely 144
  medicinal use 67
  planting 34
  tea 63
sweet flag 77
sweet woodruff 121
Symphytum officinale See
  comfrey

t

Tanacetum balsamita See
  costmary
  T. parthenium See
    feverfew
  T. vulgare See tansy

tansy 177
    companion plants for 37
    for decoration 69
    planting 34
    positioning 15
Taraxacum officinale See
    dandelion
tarragon
    French 62, 90
    kitchen gardens 14
    Russian 90
tea, herb 63–64, 138, 139,
    140, 143, 159, 160, 185
tender herbs 24
textures in garden herbs
    13
theme garden herbs 19–20
thistle, blessed 104
thyme 180–1
    collecting 57, 58
    culinary use 65
    companion plant for 37
    creeping, division 51
    groundcover 23, 44

kitchen gardens 14
lawns 22
medicinal use 67
parterres 19
paths 23
positioning 14-15
scented 20, 72
soil for pots 12
for special places 21
types 13
uses 60
walls 23
wheel garden 18
Thymus spp. *See* thyme
tincture 68
tofu, herbs for 63
tomato sauce, herbs for 63
tools and equipment
    39–40, 43
topiary herbs 13
Tropaeolum majus See
    nasturtium
tropical herbs 24
trowels 40

U, V

Urtica dioica See stinging
    nettle
USDA hardiness zones
    24–25
uses for herbs 60–74
valerian 184
    hedges 23
    red 100
Valeriana officinalis See
    valerian
velvet plant *See* mullein
Verbascum thapsus See
    mullein
Verbena officinalis See
    vervain
vervain 186
Vinca major See
    periwinkle
    V. minor See
    periwinkle
vinegars, herb 60–61
Viola spp. *See* violet

violet 187
    disease 49
    to encourage wildlife 74
    medicinal use 67

W, Y

walls herbs in 23
warts 67, 179
watercress 144
watering 45
    containers 12, 22
    tools 40
weed control 42–43
weight loss 136
wheel garden herbs 18
wildlife, herbs
    encouraging 74
willow, white 163
    for headache 66, 163
    propagation 51
    uses 60
windowboxes for
    container herbs 12

winter protection 46–47
winter savory, culinary
    use 62
witch hazel
    for cosmetic use 20
    propagation 51
    uses 60
wormwood, companion
    plant for 37
wreaths 69, 70
wrinkle cream 167
yarrow 76
    planting 34

acknowledgments

My education as an herb gardener began at my mother's knee, searching out dandelions for a spring tonic and tying snippets of lavender into my father's handkerchiefs for sachets. I didn't realize what a thorough grounding I was getting in precious lore until decades later, when I would mention some such pastime to gardening friends, only to be met by blank stares. Didn't everybody know that chamomile worked better than expensive shampoos for making your hair gleam? Was I the only one that made my own teas instead of buying fancy boxed blends? For that early head start, I have to say, Thanks, Mom.

Gratitude goes to Jimmie Epler, too, who taught me the basics of botany over several seasons of outdoor jaunts, until I knew a mustard from a phlox without taking an exploratory nibble. Arch Judd taught me the importance of learning Latin, and gave me immersion lessons at his dinner table, where only botanical nomenclature was spoken. Lessons are everywhere, though, once you start asking questions, and I am also thankful for the many seasoned gardeners and practitioners who generously shared what they knew, whether by chance encounter in the woods or a long visit over the backyard fence. Lastly, Charlotte Beech, the editor of this book, is as rare a find as that elusive blue Himalayan poppy—her editorial eye and ear for language are as sharp as her sense of humor, which kept me laughing throughout. And that, as even herb gardeners will agree, is the best medicine.

picture credits

Page 10/11 Andrew Lawson RHS Chelsea 1999 Designer Terence Conran, **12** Derek St Romaine RHS Hampton Court 1999 Designed by Ruth Chivers, **16** Jules Selmes, **17** Glyn Barton, **21** Derek St Romaine RHS Chelsea 1998 Designed by Bunny Guiness, **24** David Murray, **26/27** Clive Nichols/Tonie Lewenhaupt Sweden, **28** (bot) David Murray, **35** Derek St Romaine RHS Chelsea 1994 Designed by Noula Hancock and Matthew Bell, **38** (left) Claire Nuridsany and Marie Perennou /SPL, **39** David Murray, **49** (top) Rex Butcher/GPL, **49** (mid) Howard Rice/GPL, **49** (bot) Lamontagne/GPL, **50** David Murray, **52** Derek St Romaine, **57**(right) Lamontagne/GPL, **86, 89** (top), & **91** David Murray, **95** Derek St Romaine, **98/9** J S Sira/GPL, **100, 101,** & **106/7** David Murray, **108** Andrew Lawson, **114/5** Howard Rice/GPL, **118, 123** (top), **125,** & **129** David Murray, **141** John Glover/GPL, **146** David Murray, **152** Derek St Romaine, **163** David Murray, **172** William Gray/Oxford Scientific Films, **174 & 178** David Murray